# Climate Change
## The Facts, Impacts and Remedies

**By**
Sachin Ramar

* * * * *

## Copyright © 2019

## This book is available in print at most online retailers.

# Table of Contents

# Table of Contents

# Table of Contents

# Introduction

Imagine that you were asked to mention some of the leading global catastrophe that is threatening life on the planet earth, how would you answer? You'd need no racking of the brain to mention social, political, and economic crisis. But would you by chance pick "environmental crisis?"

Only a few would do too! And if you did, then you deserve an applaud. Nevertheless, you would still be required to dive deeper into aspects of the environmental crisis.

Climate change, which is one of these environmental crises threatens all life on the planet earth, including non-living things; we are all subjects to its detrimental effect.

Unfortunately, some individuals aren't informed as regards the damage climate change can bring, owing to falsified information, or intentional alteration of information, and progressively, these have led to myths encircling the subject, climate change.

Touched by these inaccuracies, I'm compelled to present facts about climate change. The points to be displayed comes from scientific perspective to secure the possession of well-informed knowledge.

To accomplish the primary goal of this piece, which is to present facts and accurate information concerning climate change, updated figures would be embedded into each effect of climate change and how to remedy the unfortunate occurrence.

Effects on Human, animals, water - ocean, sea life, agriculture and food supply, economy, and seasons would be extensively discussed. Furthermore, solutions would also be featured in the book, most especially "adaption," which is a crucial concept of climate change.

But, let's begin by explaining vividly, the subject itself; let's get to know it. Thus, you can answer the question: What is climate change?

## What is Climate Change?

To begin with, it' s vital that I clear off this misconception about climate change and global warming. Although, often, I see people taking these concepts as synonyms. But are they so? The answer is no!

It should be noted that global warming results in climate change; thus, you could correctly say that one of the causes of climate change is global warming.

But how could that be so? As the temperature of the planet earth rises beyond its regular natural rise, the climate in turns varies.

Notwithstanding, it is believed that earth's temperature (warming up and getting colder) has in its natural state in the last epoch been occurring taking millions of years, and the cycle has always been nearly insignificant, that is slowly, without noticeable change. Nevertheless, in less than two centuries, 200 years, earth's temperature has rapidly been changing, which when investigated, such occurrence in the past results into extinction.

With the points explained above, Climate change results when the changes, seen and experienced in the earth's climate system leads to an entirely new weather pattern that would last more than a decade or in worst case scenario, last for millions of years.

And sadly, this affects the five known parts of the climate system — namely, the atmosphere, hydrosphere, biosphere, lithosphere, and cryosphere.

As briefly highlighted, global warming is a significant culprit for climate change, which brings about ill results on the physical, biological and the entire human system amidst others minor effects.

Global warming results from a natural process called the greenhouse effect, where the atmosphere preserves some of the sun's heat, letting the earth retains all needed for the life's survival. Without it, the earth's temperature would be -18°c, which definitely wouldn't host life.

If this natural process wouldn't be altered, it's still a blessing to life. But the reverse is the case. Human activities have influenced, developed the natural method; they have maximized the greenhouse effect, which leads to a significant increase in the earth's temperature.

Aside from the increase of the greenhouse effect, other causes behind global warming include deforestation, destruction of marine ecosystems, and population increase.

But, one big question is, must you be keen about the subject, or just put, why should you learn about climate change? Let's get the answer in the preceding paragraphs.

## Why Should You Care About Climate Change?

More than ever before, this is the right time to care about climate change. Why? First and foremost, be informed that scientists all over the world are working tirelessly tracking more significant storms, droughts that are lasting more than usual time frame, and intense heat. If these aren't cared for, will they mean well for humans? Absolutely no!

Furthermore, the intense weather falls back on the ocean, increasing its evaporation, meeting the already warmed atmosphere, it tends to hold the water, resulting in instability. From stronger heat waves to an increase in the storm surge and rapid growth in the snowfall. In fact, from 1970 till date, natural disasters have taken a firm hold of the world's event, to the point that more than 85% of natural disasters are weather-related, and what is the cause? Climate Change! To what effect? Damage of life and property!

Think about the coral reefs that are going extinct, the forest that is losing their relevance, arctic animals that are missing their place of comfort, the threats on infrastructure, health, agriculture, water supply and other essential parts that are being attacked by climate change.

But there is good news! Good news? Yes, even though the damaging effect of climate change is horrible, we can solve it, yes, we can resist it. And how?

Although concerted efforts would have a far-reaching effect, within your capacity, this book will teach and guide you on how you can do it. You will realize that this is the best time to act the most, the part that demands urgency.

The remaining parts of this book would serve as an eye opener to that. But before I delve into the long-lasting solutions, I'll love to elucidate on the effects, some of which affects us directly.

As you read, pay attention to the scientific facts and figures. Note that this book isn't to create terror or fear. Instead, it is to serve as a source of reliable information on climate change.

Now, let's talk about how rooted climate change is frightening man's existence.

# Chapter 1

# Climate Change and Human Existence

## Overview

Climate change is a substantial danger to human life, it affects what we consume, the atmospheric condition we feel, and the air we breathe in. Some of the effects of climate change that results into these impacts are alteration in precipitation, rising sea levels, warming temperatures, and the force of some acute weather event. When these are altered it results in instability!

However, how swift we swing into action in tackling these dangers would either maximize the gravity or reduce the negative impacts that will be done. Additionally, changes felt by individual are subjects to one's sex, age, economic level and general attitude of such individuals. Moreover, where an individual resides, the level of exposure to the climate change, a person's sensitivity to the threats that it presents, and finally, the level of action put in place within the set where the threat is being experienced would influence how severe the risk would be.

Take, for instance, the region in which an individual stay. An individual staying in a growing country would be highly liable to health associated risk of exposure to climate change. In developed regions, the impact is not much, but yet, they still wrestle different classes of individuals. These include children, poor people, aged adults, and conceived women.

For more clarifications, I'll highlight some of the reports that buttress the fact that climate change has an impact on human health even in developed countries or region.

Barely three years ago, in 2016, a survey from the Global Change Research program reveals that even in the United States, there is a notable impact of climate change. For example, it has stand to put the health of Americans into acute risk. Their health is being affected in two ways. One, climate change can make the already existed health problems to become more severe, and two, it can lead to unforeseen development of health problems. These occurrences could be in the region where they've never existed.

Furthermore, the UN reports that climate change would, more than ever before in the future worsen health risks which will be a bad hit on the populations. There are five enlightened facts shared that it is worth revealing. They are:

*Sensitivity.* Although everyone is liable to the harmful negative impacts of climate change, our sensitivity can make a difference on how rapid, the effect could be. Children, pregnant woman, migration status, poverty, associated health risk increase susceptibility. So, if you aren't of these classes you still have a low rate of the hit, but you aren't free.

*New Health Issues Would Surface.* It is said that climate change is capable of bringing about new health issues. Stress from heat is capable of making working condition difficult and unbearable. Thus, in the face of that, more chronic ailments emerge like renal and other types of diseases. Additionally, more people, more than 20 million are annually being displaced, either by climate itself or by weather associated disasters. These figures are on the increase day in day out.

*Under-nutrition And Malnutrition.* In growing regions especially, climate change affects food quality. Apart from that, some would not even have much to eat. Food security tends to be a significant problem in countries around Latin America, Africa, and other Asia countries.

*Water-borne Diseases.* The openness of this water-borne disease to climate change is indeed a threat to human life. An example of this waterborne disease is diarrhea. Sadly, both in developed and developing countries climate change has influenced the spread.

*Transmission of Diseases Is on The Rise.* Dengue is a disease that threatens a whole lot of people today. Climate change will help in expanding it globally, thus increasing the susceptibility of some people.

The distribution is being influenced by climate change more often and rapidly.

Despite the attacks to health that climate change brings, the risk can still be minimized. Several strategies could be employed either for adapting or mitigating to prevent people from dying or avoiding the illness. It awesomely preserves the future generation and our environment at large.

While mitigation explains actions adopted to reduce, limit greenhouse gas emissions or get rid of carbon from the atmosphere. Adaptation in its broad term, means actions taken to minimize the detrimental impact either to the health of an individual or the environment at large.

Picking the impact to health one after the other, we can have insight into what could be done to limit one's exposure and how liable one is to the ill effects. Let's start from the air quality impact that climate change brings to human.

### Air - Quality

Undeniably, the air we inhale is being affected by changes in the climate. Regardless of where we are staying - indoor or outdoor. Be reminded that climate change, in turn, results in an alteration in the temperature and weather pattern, that is, the temperature becomes warmer, while weather shifts more often and rapidly. This alteration can increase the risk of an individual to asthma, cardiovascular health impact, and other respiratory diseases.

Also, droughts which is an impact from climate change make bushes vulnerable to wildfire attack. This leads to more smokes in the atmosphere, polluting the air; we tend to be more liable to the severe attack and damage of inhaling toxic air. This also increases the level of carbon dioxide in the atmosphere impacts airborne allergens.

The U.S., air quality is even under attack even in the face of consistent improvement since its initial launch in the year 1970's. Some Americans who live in some province have not yet been able to meet up with the standard of air breathed in. Sadly, climate change is making it harder to meet that standard even in the coming future, and as a result, more people are exposed to hazardous air. Another critical aspect of air quality impact is the rise in the ozone, changes in particulate matter, and changes in allergens.

Modern science has predicted that warmer temperature is emanating from climate change which means one has to battle unhealthy stages of ground-level ozone. Consider these few points:

Those exposed to a substantial level of ground-level ozone are placed at higher risk of either premature death or being diagnosed with a respiratory problem; a problem that might need them to visit the hospital more often!

Many days with poor air quality would continually be on the increase because warm and static air will increase how the ozone forms, climate change, in turn, will then increase the levels of ground-level ozone in previously polluted areas.

The impact of ground-level ozone is toxic. It can lead to lung tissue damage; it limits lung function and could cause airways inflammation. In fact, in some cases, it has resulted in the aggravation of asthma and several other respiratory issues. Therefore, folks with this issue are already at higher risk.

At any increase in ozone concentrations as a result of climate change, changes will influence the already existing ozone-related ailments. Which will, unfortunately, leads to more death toll.

**The other aspect: Changes in the particulate matter.**

The term used in describing the liquid droplets and tiny particles in the atmosphere suspended in the atmosphere is called "particulate matter." Let's see how it affects air quality.

This small particle is usually around 2.5 micrometers. These types include dust, naturally and artificially occurring sea spray, and wildfire smoke. When fossil fuels are being burned to generate energy, it serves an inclusion to the presence of particulate matter suspended in the atmosphere.

There are two ways in which this chemical could get to the final stage. They can be directly emitted into the atmosphere or on reaching the atmosphere they form from chemical reactions such as nitrogen dioxide, sulfur oxide, and several other volatile organic compounds.

**The health impact of these are highlighted below:**

If intentionally or unintentionally a person inhales any of these tiny particles, it will harm the health of the person; it will lead to lung cancer, cardiovascular and pulmonary diseases.

The intensity 0f wildfire is influenced by climate change. How? Particulate matter found in the wildfire smoke can be transported a long distance by wind, and this affects anyone near this air pollutant.

For the older ones, they have a particular sensitivity to short-term particle exposure. Thus, their risk of hospitalization is being increased, and even in the worst-case scenario, death.

Outdoor workers too, are more exposed than those bedridden. Their exposure is times two of those in the hospitals.

Notwithstanding, it should be understood that several factors alter the atmospheric levels of tiny particulate matter, but the one thing is they are involved, and as a result, it is difficult to predict whether there will likely be a decrease or increase in the concentration, years to come. Gladly, some of the particulate matter can be gotten rid by rainfall.

**The final part is the changes in the allergens and asthma triggers.**

Since climate change can pose threats to the respiratory organs, it thereby can aggravate already existing respiratory disease. And from the current data gotten from scientific research, it is seen that air pollution, a result of climate change can lead to asthma.

For people with allergies, data collected between the year 1995 and 2011, the warmer temperatures in the U.S., have made the pollen season to have an increase, at least 15- 25 days longer. That explains how warmer temperatures can lead to blooming flowers and then it will result in the emission of carbon dioxide. Then this change will lead to an increase in the concentration of air leading to the strength of airborne allergens and finally increasing the symptoms of allergy. With this process, anyone without allergies may develop one.

Anyone currently battling with allergies and asthma can win the war, they can reduce their risks and ultimately reduce the impact that climate change can have on them.

1. ***Meet Your Doctor.*** One of the best approaches to take is to meet a qualified doctor that understands 85% of the impact of climate change on the air quality, he will evidently give some restrictions and for better health management, adhere strictly to the instructions.

2. ***Avoid Exposures to Areas of likely Trigger.*** One of the instructions or avoidance that might be given to you is that you should avoid constant exposure to an area that can trigger an attack or an allergic reaction.

3. ***Check the Air Quality Index (AQI).*** Air quality index is adopted, and it is being used to report daily air quality. It is this index that will allow you to know if the air in a region is clean or polluted and the health effects that you are liable to. The chart has several categories. From good to moderate, unhealthy for sensitive skins, and hazardous. Accordingly, it is excellent that before you move out of your home check this quality to see how high your risk is. If your rick is high, it is excellent to restrain yourself from this air impact when you restrict some outdoor activities.

If you'd want to enjoy the flawless functioning of your respiratory organs, I will advise that you stick to these three steps discussed above.

There is another way climate change affects a person's health. It is the mental aspect of one's health. This aspect, mental health, should be given great concern too. It is significant to discuss this aspect, in fact limiting the environmental impact on health is valuable as understanding the effect it does to the mental health.

## Mental Health

Most of the research made regarding the impact of climate change on health often exclude mental health. In this sub-topic, I'll be highlighting succinctly how climate change impacts mental health and what recent research has to offer so we can have a fundamental understanding of the topic.

When a natural disaster, one resulting from the impact of climate change strikes, there are numerous psychological effects. The damages and trauma featured in media coverage of the crash are often terrifying.

Pain and injuries that emanate from loss of properties and loved ones leave a more significant impact on the life of the individual that is being affected. As this condition continues to change in frequency and severity, these types of experiences should be well understood and how best to mitigate the situation should be learned.

It is examined that when intense weather events occur, increased in the depression, anxiety, and post-traumatic stress disorder are felt. It becomes even worse when there is little or no warning signal, and they are just met unprepared.

However, it is not that climate change is responsible for the development of the new mental disorder, but it exposes people to a situation that can expose them to possible aggravation. That is, they have once had the problem, but now the incident would trigger it even more.

I will be using an authentic life experience in clarifying the point above. A man named Rico is battling with a regular increase in mental illness as a result of family issues and poverty, and relatives and friends of Rico know this. But after the hit of Hurricane Maria in September 2017, his mental problem got intensified that he asked to seek more medical attention.

Also, climate change also causes a hindrance to the recovery process of a mental health patient. It can slow down and halt the healing process temporarily. It could displace and put them apart from their medications and drugs. Interestingly, damages recorded from climate change are not always instantaneous. They are sometimes gradual, leaving the aftermath to be felt on ecosystems and landscape. This can then lead to loss too for those with a knitted relationship with the environment.

Sadly, a report even discloses that warming temperature leads to the suicides of more than 50,000 individuals in India during these three decades. It should also be noted that a slight change or alteration in a person's physical health can have a terrible impact on their mental health.

Here are three crucial facts to always remember when it comes to the relationship between mental health and climate change.

1. ***People with mental illness are often time susceptible to intense heat***. In fact, in a recent survey, an already reported case of mental illness possess the risk of death at the alteration of the temperature, resulting in heat waves. Also, anyone administered drug for mental issues would be at risk since their medications can bring about the difficulty in regulating body temperature.

2. ***Those who do not have any record of mental illness can still be affected.*** By the news report displayed on the TV regarding the strike of climate change. It can influence how the brain responds to stress.

3. Children, older adults, pregnant women, people with existing mental illness issues, emergency workers, and low-income earners are at higher risk for mental health. It impacts them the more.

Apart from the mental health illness that climate change presents to every individual, it also operates at the community level. The stages, frequency has elevated hostility, loss of social identity, interpersonal aggression. Affected communities will experience inappropriate mental health impacts.

There are several ways of wrestling the impact at both individual and community level. It is incredible if a person suffering from the psychological effect can build resilience. Below are five points that can aid in recovering from the trauma felt from the impact.

1. ***Build Relieve in Resilience.*** To recover quickly, you need hope, active hope. You have to do things that would make it sure that you want to transcend from the region of the trauma to acceptance then taking steps that would make you recover like helping others or creating long term goals that would make you think less about your loss.

2. ***Be Optimistic.*** Fostering the spirit of optimism is indeed a way to move on. It tells you that thing will be better, that the condition is temporary, and indeed it is.

3. ***Develop Active Coping and Self-regulation Skills.*** During any period of grief, pain, and discomfort, you need to create a strategy that helps you cope faster. Acquire skills that will allow you to dwell minimally on your current situation.

4. ***Invest in Connectivity.*** There are places you can get motivations, from family and friends. Try and build a connection with these categories of people. The excellent conversation, the in-depth laughter will help lessen your anxiety level; remember that they will give words of hope to assist in restoring your condition.

5. ***Pursue a Meaningful Life***. Begin by asking yourself what brings meaning to your life. You should be very objective here because your critical thinking will reinforce positive vibe, which is impressive in giving you the best therapy and pill.

Going by these five options, getting past your trauma in less time is achievable.

Finally, you should be informed that climate change has a diversity of ways. It could either be direct, indirect or more. Apart from what an individual could do in addressing the problem, the community as a whole has more to do so that they are adequately treated.

Also, in solving it in the community sector, there must be the adoption of transformative action where all the active hope is well harnessed and explained, where communities as a whole are mobilized.

At the stage, it is imperative to consider how climate change impacts the temperature and how it affects human. Aside from the mentioning of rising in the temperature, you need to know how it connects to human. Moving you speedily and precisely, the impact of temperature is what we have below.

**Temperature Impact**

From the onset, I've talked about how climate change impacts temperature. But that is not all there is when it comes to the impact on temperature and how it tends to affect man in its fuller sense and scale. Climate's constant change hits the global temperature and makes it warm, and the culprit is the heat-trapping greenhouse gas emissions from human impact.

Presently, in Massachusetts, there is a significant increase in the level of temperature. The temperature has become faster and higher, to the point that the heat has grown faster than the experience we have in the global rates. Surprisingly, the last rise was felt in the year 1895, and an increase of 2.8°F is way too high. And if something is not done to reduce greenhouse gas emissions drastically, the tendency of temperatures warming from 6 up to 10° F at the end of the century.

This increase might not seem to you like an issue; after all, it's a little figure. But for proper understanding permit me to breakdown what a degree is, or better asked what makes up a degree?

**What Makes up a Degree?**

The small change I said earlier in the temperature stands for a long-term replacement for the whole world. To help you see how significant those figures are, in the last iceberg, the temperature was only 9° cooler comparing to what we have today.

And then, the current New England was all wrapped by glaciers 3,000 feet thick. For a closer and more precise picture, the same changes of temperature seen from an iceberg till date could occur during the lifetime of children given birth to in the 21 century. So devastating!

As it stands, if no actions are taken to remedy the situation, we will discover that the so-called minute increase will lead to a significant improvement in temperature.

Another point to note about climate change impact on temperature is that warmer temperature will give rise to more extreme heat. It is no lie that currently we experience warmth at its peak. The more temperature is being disturbed, the more dangerous we are likely to be affected by a heat wave.

It is troubling that Boston experiences 11 days of 90 ° F every year now. And by 2020, if not curbed, it could extend beyond that, making it be from 20 to 90 days with a very high degree that goes beyond 100°F.

Also, temperature impact leads to longer growing seasons and diminishing winter. Currently, in the northeast, the growing season has increased. Falls are approaching very late. And for springs, the change makes it warmer, and summer comes soon. The only expectation is that the changes will be increasing and accelerate rapidly. Unfortunately, the end of this century could bring about a cold season which will become one month or two months shorter.

Even though to some reasonable degree growing season could mean good in some ways, the Massachusetts town entirely relies on the moderate and balanced dose of snow every winter to create less time for snow to hang around.

Other aspects of temperature related impact increase death-related issues reaching the united states and other countries by the end of the century in the months of summer.

Favorably, the use of air conditioning has been experimented to reduce the death toll, by saving people from extreme heat. Interestingly, the use of air conditioning is one of the adaptive responses.

Regular exposure to extreme heat is liable to lead folks to stroke and acute dehydration. Including are cerebrovascular diseases and other respiratory diseases. Closely affected are populations located in the northern latitudes because over there, there is less information, and then they are not even prepared, and coping becomes something off-sight.

Also, apart from the regional impact. The type of occupation, your likes and other factors are playing a significant role. Workers that stay outside more often, students that engage in athlete outside the sun, homeless people are more exposed to extreme heat. Therefore, they are at high risk. That is not all though.

Individual with no access to air conditioner but stay indoor more often are the object of the target too, since their exposure to heat is being increased more often. People with health-related issues are also at risk since there would be difficulty in the body regulating the temperature itself.

Also, for those staying in the rural settlement, they are less likely to be affected, although there will be still be change, they have a lesser risk when compared to those staying in the urban areas where the atmosphere there is often warmer in contrast to the rural settlement. When heat waves knock at these centers, they are the ones to be first affected, and they are at such vulnerable to other forms of health-related impact.

During a period of heat way, the partner, stagnant air makes air pollution becomes more evident and then other health associated impacts are nearly unavoidable.

As a bonus, I want to show you three of the strong evidence that shows that air is getting warmer.

1. Half a decade ago, the number of cold days in various locations had gotten down, and it is being replaced by most places worldwide.

2. *Since the era of 1880, the year 2001 down to 2010 is known to be the warmest in the history of man.* During those years, temperature records became available globally; this leads to a more straightforward calculation of the global average.

3. Though subject to the amount of carbon emits, by the end of the century, the average calculated global temperature is set to get an increase between 3.1 - 7.2 ° F

As an individual your task here is to embrace these three leading solutions: *adopting greening transportation, ensuring the excellent management of forest and agriculture and reviving up Renewables.* Doing that is a simple effort, it gets you somewhere.

If after ensuring that quality air is breathed in, the right level of temperature is maintained. The food we consumed, one of the most critical aspects of life needs serious concern. Climate change still hits this part. But a few facts read into these aspects would offer you one of the best ways to maintain a quality life since we are what we consume.

**Food Safety and Nutrition**

But why must food feature in the climate change impacts? The direct effect of higher concentrations of carbon dioxide present in the atmosphere is enormous threats to food safety. Additionally, extreme weather condition is capable of slowing down and disrupting the distribution of food.

Since the inception of rapid climate change, new patterns of cultivation, animal diseases, humans, and crop have all possess threat on consuming a quality meal. Though, the effects of climate change on food security and nutrition can be positive or negative as it comes from temperature and precipitation. But before I step more in-depth, it's great you know the meaning of food safety or security and nutrition.

According to the definition presented by World Health Organization, Food safety is defined as when everyone everywhere at all levels and times has undeniable access to safe, sufficient and nutritious food so you can retain a healthy and more active life.

The idea behind food safety is termed physical and economic access to food that fits into people's dietary requirement. Climate change will influence good food, air, shelter and minute exposures to the rapidly evolving animals.

Take for example, since the start of the 21st century, climate change has impacted many global burdens of ailments, food, and premature death.

Malnutrition in turns comes from the direct impact of climate change on agricultural production. As a result, we can trace climate change as having an indirect effect on nutrition insecurity that bounds around us today. And in a more direct form, food availability.

Going by the definition of food security, World Food Summit defines it to be when all people, possess both physical an economic access to safe, nutritious and abundant food that touches all aspect of eating that will influence an active and healthy life.

Check deeply these four keys that food nutrition security relies on. Let's pick them one after the other.

1. *Availability.* This has to do with the presence of sufficient, high-quality food that is distributed via household production.

2. *Access.* This means the ability of an individual to get their ways through the right amount of quality food to improve the quality of food they have to feed on to get nutritional value.

3. *Utilization.* It is one thing to have the food and have access to it, another is the ability to utilize the food the best way based on feeding practices, health care practices you consulted, and access to quality water and health care services.

4. *Stability.* Stability ensures that at all time, the food is available for consumption

Climate change alters these four aspects of food safety highlighted above, and as a result, food available has some toxicity or even getting the right meal becomes a real problem.

Take a closer look at what menace climate change is causing in Pakistan. The economy of Pakistan is based on agriculture. But presently Pakistan is wrestling with a severe problem like irrigation water. This is as a result of little or excess rainfall in the region. And just like animals and human, some plants are highly sensitive — crops like rice, spices, vegetables, and cereals.

The rising and falling of temperature also lead to a shortage of water, and when this happens, there comes to be a problem of food security as a result of crop productivity. Regrettably, food insecurity can influence the growth of a country. It can hinder the economic and social development of a nation.

I have four fundamental points I will be dishing out as regards food safety and nutrition. These points are aids to better understanding.

1. *Increase in Temperature Would lead to Bacteria-Related Food Poisoning*. Salmonella, for example, is a bacteria- associated with food poisoning. The reason is since bacteria grow spontaneously in areas of warmer temperature. And unhappily, they can lead to severe diseases like gastrointestinal disease and some can even result in death in extreme

cases. As an individual, often keep your cooked meal hot, before eating, adopt all other forms of safeguarding foods even in the face of climate consistent change.

2. *Risk of Food Contaminant is High.* The higher the occurrence of the atmosphere changes the higher the risk of this form of exposure. A higher sea temperature will lead to higher mercury presence in seafood. Even during extreme weather occurrence, there will be extreme cases of contaminants into the food chain via stormwater runoff.

3. *Artificial fertilizer And Lower level of Protein.* The increase in the presence of carbon dioxide would result in compost for some variety

23

of plants and crops. Meanwhile, there will be a reduction in the protein level and other minerals that won't lead to a nutritious harvest.

4.*Inability to Distribute Food Accordingly*. The excess rainfall that leads to flooding and scarcity of rain which leads to drought affects the distribution of food as a result of damaged waterways or accessibility tends to be a significant problem.

Undeniably, the impact of climate change is disheartening. You can now trace most food poisonings to climate change, most malnutrition diet to climate change. Since, at the grass-root level, your home, you can minimize the impact, but embracing good and quality hygiene is reasonable. Cook meal thoroughly, ensure that vegetables are well boiled, meat is not exposed to excess air and eat lunch when hot.

If climate change can impact food safety, you might ask, will it have an impact on water? After all, when exposed to contaminated water, illness becomes inevitable. So, lets us see how climate change plays its part in bringing about this vital, yet must-know aspect of life.

**Water-Related Illnesses**

As this terror continues, it is speculated that the severity of weather will become more prominent and unavoidable. Most especially the rate of precipitation will experience drastic change. For some regions, they will be faced with excessive rainfall, while in some areas, what they will meet is intense drought. But a skeptic mind could wish to inquire and see how the increase in precipitation affects water quality. That is easy.

When precipitation increases, the risk of flooding becomes a significant problem. And flood is a threat to human life; it spread quickly and rapidly pathogens, and human is being exposed. More so, in developing countries, they are at risk as well, because water carries wastes to create an avenue for mosquitoes to breed. Also, the availability of water facilities is subject to attack as they become damaged and this can result in the distribution of untreated water or poorly treated water. During an increase in precipitation, the flood can cause the sewer and water pipes to break, and this can lead to contamination of drinking water.

Additionally, flooding is capable of moving fecal matter from the ground that has overflowed, and then it will lead to the contamination of wells, surface water or borehole waters.

Three categories of diseases come from floods. The first identified as waterborne diseases; an example of this one is diarrhea. The second, mosquito-borne diseases emanated from the stagnant water that gives mosquitoes an easy avenue to breed well. The last part that results from the extreme exposure to water also entails fungal skin disease, respiratory illness and finally eye infections.

Furthermore, excessive flooding can increase the rate of runoff from fields. More sediments and nutrients will then be deposited in higher quantity to the water. They will gradually move to other problems. For example, it can lead to algae blooms, and they can disturb the aquatic life that is present in water and will immensely impair the quality of the water.

Recent research shows how intense the problem is. Take for example, between the period of 1948 down to 1994, more than 250 of the over 500 disease outbreaks were as a result of an increase in precipitations. To reveal how rapid the situation is, outbreaks often becomes apparent the same month intense precipitation happens. And for contamination of groundwater, that occurs as a result of extreme rainfall; it takes two months to occur.

An outbreak called E. coli in the region of Ontario is a perfect case to use in furthering my explanation. On May 8, 2009, an increase in precipitation was recorded in the Walkerton, Ontario. The first four days experienced from 10 to 20 millimeters of rainfall, regrettably, this only happens once in every 60 years. The overburdening of the groundwater aquifers including excess water at the surface of the earth disrupt the water supply with the E. coli bacteria.

Drought in turn though only minimizes the level of runoff, but it still has a part to play. It reduces the quality of water. Since drought brings down the level of water. The concentration of sediments and minerals becomes so high and thereby affecting the quality of the water.

No doubt, people can be infected when they drink contaminated water. Aside from the previously listed ailments that could be encountered, Liver and kidney damage is one of the viable damages done to human health.

Well, water resources, environmental agencies and public health in developed countries are helping their subjects to safeguard themselves so that risk of contamination can be reduced. They have developed strategies like water quality monitoring, beach closures, several pieces of advice on how effective one has to boil water and the best way to harvest fishes, shellfish.

But, what about individuals in developing countries and underdeveloped countries? Although there is little the government and established agencies are doing regarding this, there is a solution that individual can master. These are explained below.

Although waterborne diseases are capable of causing bacteria, parasites, and viruses, there are some actions that one can take to limit the chances of contracting the water-borne illness.

1. *Good Hygiene is a Must.* One of the best ways to solve the issue. There is a need to be conscious of your health more than ever before. Be concern about what you drink, even if

you have to guzzle any drinks, be sure that the company has seal by bodies regulating water quality. When you cook, boil water to high degrees.

*2.Join Programs That promotes Safe Water Drinking.* There are varieties of educational programs that will be taught in these sessions about how you can keep yourself free from chemical contaminants. You tend to learn how water is being used; you will be informed about current water issues. There is more, you are opened to sessions that let you see health issues that result from drinking water. These programs are nice and would guarantee leading a quality life.

3. ***Teach Others.*** It is very likely that good hygiene is oblivious to your friends and family. It is your responsibility to teach such ones since through them you might be exposed to the sad result of drinking unsafe water. You can enroll your kids to programs that enlighten students on how to recognize safe water for drinking.

If everyone can live by these precautionary motives, the mortality rate would be curtailed, aside from that, quality of life can be improved. However, the impact of climate change on health doesn't operate on everyone in the same degree. My point? Some people are more vulnerable to impacts than others. But what are the factors that are responsible for the vulnerability? Having a firm understanding of the populations of concern is the roadway of answering that question.

## Populations of Concern

Several factors are responsible for the vulnerability of those exposed to the adverse effect of climate change. The consideration for each susceptibility differs. Three of this will be discussed successively.

***The first one, which is sensitivity (much on this later)*** means the rate or the level at which climate change is impacting stress on them.

***Two, which is exposure*** means the contact, physical in most cases, between an individual and the trigger or better put stressor.

***The last one, adaptive capacity*** means the ability of a person to adjust to or do away with prospective hazards.

Take this into consideration; how these three-work hand in hand. Older adults are often sensitive to intense heat. But if this individual decides to stay indoors, and with the help of an air-condition, he reduces how exposed he is to extreme weather. If he can continually manage the bills from electricity consumption, then he can gradually and confidently win the war. Taking these actions to reduce her exposure is clearly defined as the adaptive capacity he has received.

The vulnerability of an individual to climate change might be as a result of exposures or sensitivity. However, it could be as a result of both. For more clarified points check these points below.

***Children Vulnerability Are High.*** Children are often vulnerable to several health issues. And it is as a result of their biological sensitivities and exposures during outdoor activities. Besides, pregnant women are not exempted from this attack; heat waves and flooding affect them too.

***Occupational Groups That Are Vulnerable to Attacks.*** As briefly highlighted, the type of occupation you do could have an impact on your exposures. Professions like transportation workers, paramedics, outdoor workers, workers in stem houses; Vector-borne and intense heat are common exposures they will wrestle with.

***An Individual with Chronic Medical Condition Would Suffer Same Fate.*** Several medications could make accurate body regulation of intense heat difficult. Also, some bedridden individuals are compounded on electrical medical equipment for sustenance, but when there are power outages, they are volatile to attack.

***Disabled Individual Would be Impacted Too.*** For people with disabilities, during an intense weather attack, they might have to need an emergency response, and if no one could come to their aid, it can lead to more damages to their health.

***Older Adults.*** There are so many reasons why older adults would find it difficult to adapt to the situation. Two of the impacts apart from heat sensitivity and occurrence of disabilities are financial in-capabilities and preexisting medical condition.

Sensitivity Are Being Affected by a Host of Many factors; they range from higher risk of exposure, educational elements, the intense prevalence of the medical condition, socioeconomic, they also impact adaptive capacity.

Regardless of the impact and problem they could bring. There is viable relief those with sensitivity and exposure can enjoy; they can regain their healthy number routine. Mapping out the strategies to reduce the vulnerability, building resilience, poverty redress is sure a point to be discussed.

***Perform Vulnerability Assessment.*** This is done to carry out resilience plans. As seen, the poor are vulnerable to the effects of natural disasters — the first approach to reducing vulnerability is to affirm that it exists. And the way to verify that is by conducting the test. The primary analysis would focus on the exposure and sensitivity of biophysical systems while the more comprehensive one will include assessment of climate risk which provides for the social, ecosystem and economic vulnerability.

***Adopt Uncertainty in Resilience Planning.*** When you make plans for adaptation, getting accurate information on weather is very important. So, gather both long-term and short-term weather report and apply it in making the decision on how to reduce vulnerability. Nevertheless, remember that the weather forecast these days are becoming uncertain; it is not so sure how much rain will fall. Therefore, when planning for a reduction in vulnerability, learn to include several uncertainties about the weather. This allows for flexibility. You are fully armed with several scenarios that could come up. Having different situations helps planners to ruminate about different options and how they can implement them accordingly.

***Socially Excluded and Poor Folks Should be Featured in Decision Making.*** Since most poor peoples are the most vulnerable to the impact of climate change. If included, they can influence how accurate the result they will get. The disabled, women, elderly, and slum dwellers have little participation and influence over the allocation of resources. For countries that have higher levels of poor people who have been sidetracked, the lower socioeconomic resilience. Therefore, there is a need for more effective climate change tackling.

*They are consistently monitoring, Evaluating and Continual Learning What Works.* This is a beautiful way to keep track of the addition of adaptation plans and a way to access how effective the outcomes are. This stage is highly relevant to helping them track the success record. And happily, many countries are focusing on adaptation and embracing the attitude of monitoring, evaluating will aid in knowing what exactly will work both now and in the future. It will reduce wasted effort and help see when more time should be spent on.

*Note the Successful Adaptation Process.* I'm not saying that adaptation is the only and accurate way to solve the problem of climate change of population of concern, however, if a particular adaptation reveals that it would be of benefit to the vast majority of people to help in curating a strong resilience and limiting vulnerability, they should be noted.

Using the strategies discussed above, the government can reduce people's exposure and sensitivity, if merge with the help they could act as individual try on their part.

As you have gone through the impact of climate change on temperature, air, food, water, and mental health. You could be curious to know if that is all there is about the impact on man. While it is essential to note these five are the significant impacts, there exist other implications for health. Knowing these would assist in helping you curb their effects on you.

## Other Health Effects

From the onset of this chapter we've been highlighting how climate change is eating deep into human health, we've seen the impact on allergy, respiratory system, cardiovascular, waterborne, vector-borne diseases. But that is not all the effect.

Climate change is a crucial topic, one that brings together great men. It's what heads of state gather together to discuss about. And this convincingly tells us that there are many threats to human life, even at an international level, and for this century, it is one of the most significant risks that befall us.

Sadly, recent figures from WHO suggests a deadly hit in the nearest future; annually, from 2030 down to 2050, the rate of death from climate change would be so surmountable, a total number of 250,000 death yearly will be recorded. The causes of death from climate change would go beyond those health impacts highlighted about; there will be more.

A further breakdown shows that there definitely would be other health impacts of climate change on health aside from the previously aforementioned. Record says that 48,000 deaths from the 250,000 will be as a result of diarrhea, 95,000 from undernourishment of children, 60,000 from malaria, and 38,000 to exposures to heat among elderly ones.

Did you notice that from the figure malaria and undernourishment took the more substantial part of the forecast? Is that sending any signal?

Honestly, the direct impact of climate change, which are extreme events, drought, and flooding lead to stress, but there is also another indirect impact like the spread of diseases, post-traumatic disorder, and population displacement.

As changes in climate continue, the impact will never end. Our lovely home, the planet will be placed under harsh condition and even in the future. And in the coming years, land degradation is imminent. And the falling of agricultural land is much. And this can result in receding water resources. Sadly, the distance between available resources and water could reach a peak of over 40%, and this can lead to an inability to feed and thus impacting their health.

Migration of people in the world could also be impacted by climate change. For instance, by the year 2020, more than 60 million people would have migrated from one region to another. That is, from the part with climate change impact to areas that are less likely affected now and in the future. And this would pose a massive threat to the unhealthy global immigration problem.

I'll be focusing attention on a few of the health impact on health. Let's take vector-borne disease first. Then we will move to seasonal viruses and what could be done to fight the issue.

## Vector Borne Diseases

As defined by the medical line, vector-borne diseases are ailments or illnesses that are transmitted from one individual to the other individual by carriers. With an increase in climate change, mosquitoes are continually spreading geographically, with the inclusion of some other diseases like dengue and other viral illnesses like chikungunya.

Presently, scientists have speculated that dengue disease would become more rampant in the coming future because dengue-carrying mosquito transmitting the infection has hit an increase of 9.4% since early 1950. A close example bringing this to life is what happened in Cambodia, one of the Asian countries where the longer rainy season led to a surge in the spread of malaria.

## Seasonal Disease

There are seasonal diseases that come and go! Flu, an example of the virus cannot withstand intense temperature, the instability of the heat and due to that, they don't last a long time. Instead, they endure just a short period. Nevertheless, it must be noted that a simple difference in seasons has a higher potential of letting temperature stays constant. If that would be the case, seasonal illness could have a home to take as an abode, bringing about more widespread in the coming years, which would be disastrous to one's health.

These two illnesses that are being discussed need to be fought. We have to do something about it. Else by the final part of the century, there will be an alarming consequence on earth. Frightening consequences? Yes!

If greenhouse gas emissions are not curbed, global temperature will be on the rise and would be more than 4.5°C leading to the deadly consequences. Therefore, the present challenge, what we have to fight is limiting the increase in the temperature to 2°C.

To fight it, do not forget some of the practical measures discussed like embracing cleaner sources of energy and increasing the use of public vehicles, limiting your exposures to the already polluted atmosphere to help reduce your vulnerability to air pollution.

Regardless of what an individual can do, international organizations are also ever ready to keep increasing the awareness of their carbon footprint. They have been succeeding in achieving that via planet mobilization program. Some government agencies are fighting the unfavorable impact of climate change, and more actions are being placed to monitor the life-cycle of a product being manufactured.

Conclusively, climate change is tormenting man's existence, even though the results in some region are often subtle, everyone has the right to know. From knowing, collective efforts would mean tactfully and smartly combating it.

With this exclusive explanation of the impact of climate change on human, you should be fully armed, not caught unaware of the deadly effect. Since humans aren't the only beneficiary of the planet earth, what about other life, are they in any form being affected?

Aside humans that are wrestling the sad consequences of climate change, animals too are not immune to the impact. Populations of species are not slowly declining, but rapidly.

The next chapter, which exclusively discusses the impact of climate change on the animal will presents figures and data, from effects to sea life, land animals, extinction, migrations, and how to be more environmentally friendly with both wild and domestic animals.

**Chapter Two**

# The Impact of Climate Change on Animals

## Why Must I care?

From the previous chapter, I've comprehensively highlighted the brutal and horrible impact of climate change on human life; unfortunately, man isn't the only one suffering from this, animals do too.

Industrial actions, burning of fossil fuels, and deforestation make changes in the climate noticeable! And more extensively, it has an impact on animals. This places many species of animals at very high risk of extinction. If that is the case, who shouldn't care about this?

Simply put, the earth's ecosystem is intricately designed thus leading to complexity. So, when one plant or animal is being disturbed and affected adversely by any negative change, others would undoubtedly be affected, even human too can be affected. But why?

Remember that humans too are dependent on this same environment for survival. Our need for food, water, and resources are designed in this same environment. Therefore, any change in animals would directly be felt by humans too.

Furthermore, having a more in-depth understanding of the effect of climate change on animals isn't just vital for the preserving of species that are susceptible to the heinous impact of climate change, but it keeps human population and wildlife at peace, rather than having a conflict as a result of insufficient resources.

Regardless of our level of exposures, knowledge, and awareness about climate change's impact on animals, we all should care about it. And below are eight good reasons why you should be more keen about the effects on animals.

1. *Polar Bears and Snow Leopards Are Incredible.* Undeniably, climate change is a negative hit on animals found around the globe.

Climate change decreases their chances of getting food, water and other resources for survival. Hence, whenever there is an alteration in the weather, they, in turn, search for survival, thus decreasing their habitat. Polar bears and leopards, whose habitat are identical would have and notice a drastic change. From forest down to the ice, down to rivers and so on. And this can lead to their extinction. No! We don't just want to hear that!

2. *Coral Reef Are Awesome*. The effect of climate change will make it so difficult for coral reef to survive. In the search for survival, the stress undergone would bleach their color, leading to death. Also, when there is an increase in the C02 in the atmosphere, the situation becomes even worse. It spells doom for this beautiful creature. For coral reef to locate Nemo becomes even harder, since their beautiful and elegantly home crumbles.

It is researched that as at present the ocean is 26% more toxic, acidic. And this has led to the bleaching of the great reef! If you'd desire to see the reef one day, it might be impossible, if this terror continues.

3. *We Also Depend on Clean Air*. While the human impact of climate change progresses, it makes it so difficult for animals to enjoy a non-heavy air, a clean air to breathe in. The continued emission into the atmosphere all makes quality air becomes scarce. They have an adverse effect, undoubtedly, the severe ailments in animals, resulting in death. For humans, chances of having asthma, lung diseases and heart diseases are on the rise.

As a matter of urgency, this condition, anthropogenic climate change has made developed countries like the U.K., dub this issue "PHE (Public Health Emergency).

4. *We Need to Think About the Future Generations*. Every right-thinking human should often be concerned about what the future holds. Presently, we are still a bit fortunate to live in this beautiful, awesome planet. The great question is, do our kids deserve the same treatment? They do need to.

But how will that happen when beautiful and delicate species in the ecosystem have gone extinction due to the adverse effect of climate change? If we want the future generation to benefit, have a vibrant ecosystem to thrive, our combined effort will undoubtedly preserve these lives.

5. *We All Need Clean Water.* When placed in ratio, 9 out of 10 people are residing in areas where we have severe water scarcity. Isn't that alarming? Worse yet, when there exists a disturbance in the global temperature, let's say, it increases, it is highly liable to an increase in the water available, leading to drought and water scarcity.

This would also affect the rainfall pattern. Thus, flooding and drought would occur more often and more severe. Animals would migrate to a location where they could find sufficient water, and this can tend to conflict between humans and animals. Why? Since man too would be in search of adequate water.

6. *Everyone is Involved.* Rajendra Pachauri, chairman of the ICPP, made a clear and obvious point that no single person on the planet earth would be untouched, unharmed from the adverse effect of climate change.

You should be aware climate's change effect isn't sparingly, as mentioned briefly above, when animals are affected, we are too! Severe weather influences prices of commodities, less appreciation for the beautiful world around. Let's face it; it's a fight we have to win. A win for animals, win for humans.

7. *Bush fires and Flood Means Death for Animals.* Intense and frequent burning of bushes will precisely lead to a change in climate. For a human, bush burning can make adversely affect their health, as it would in animals. On animals, it could lead to injuries, killings, and displacement of some fame settlers. Unfortunately, this trend if not checked will continue for a very long time. Putting four-legged, furry animals at risks.

8. *Extinction is Real.* Long before now, some animals existed. The likes of dinosaurs, rhino, and others. And their destruction was influenced by asteroids and volcanoes. Today, the condition becomes even more terrible because, daily, some species of plant and animals are going extinct. The cause?

Unlike volcanoes and asteroids that influenced past knowledge, experts frantically warn that more than 90% of endangered species are going to be affected by climate change.

With these points above, have you come to the agreement that regardless of where we are, who we are, we have to be concern about the effect of climate change on an animal? Then, let's see how it operates; in the next chapter, we all exclusively talk about how climate change affects animals.

## How Climate Change Affects Animals

Seeing the need for every person to care about the impact of climate change on animals, it is imperative to know how climate change affects them, though, from the paragraphs above, you might gain a sneak pick, this sub-heading would be more explicit.

Checking into these species below, we can understand how climate change impacts animals. It would reveal to us how our biodiversity can undergo detrimental effect. As you read note that I prioritize by the adverse effect experienced by individual species of animals.

1. *How Rhinos Are Affected.* Talk of rhinos, they are already undergoing intense pressure, since it's one of the species on the planet earth that is being poached globally.

Sadly, just this last year, something happened that further shows that rhinos are experienced one of the deadly impacts of climate change, which is drought.

An example is what happened in Kenya, when drought hits Kenya, as a result of climate change, farmers records an unpredictable loss. More than 85% of the Cattles, native wildlife and black rhino, specifically, were affected.

Already, rhinos are fragile, but now, they have become even vulnerable to threats. Since the drought can bring about more poaching, locals too who need survival would have to go after their horns. The situation isn't going to become less unless something is done, until then, the drought would become more often as climates keep changing and many species will be done more endangered.

2. *How Chickless Golden Eagles Are Feeling the Impact.* Drought, being one of the adverse effects of climate change isn't the only culprit that affects an animal. Rainfall, which is also a result of climate change is responsible. It can pose the same threat.

Take, for example, birds, as a result of excessive rainfall can lead to an inability to reproduce and the overall chick production.

A more realistic example is the occurrence in west Scotland. Right there in that region, the reduction of the golden eagle population has drastically reduced by more than 25%, due to the excess rainfall in May.

Undoubtedly, we can't rule out the fact that excess rainfall, which in turn leads to flooding has negative influences on both ground-nesting birds that possess free ranging chick and mammals.

3. *How Rising Seas and Stormy Weathers Are Affecting Sea Turtles.* Sea turtles also give us a hint on climate change effects animals. The rising sea level and stormy weather wash off many of the beaches where sea turtles lay their eggs.

Moreover, the experiment shows that it is very likely that hotter sand, due to an increase in temperature would lead to sea turtle's reproduction defects since they are likely to reproduce females only. Although, this could bring about an increase in the numbers of available sea turtles. It spells disaster. How?

In the next 50 years, it is liable that the existence of warmer sand will develop into a preponderance of females which evidently would lead to the extinction of sea turtles.

Additionally, it should be noted that warmer temperature can also generate total nest failure. To what effect too? The species are becoming extinct.

4. ***What the Reduction in Sea Ice Does to Emperor Penguins.*** Though this species of penguins, the Emperor penguins is notably the most abundant species of penguins, the devastating effect of climate change is hitting them too. As a result of climate change, sea shrunk, and this leads to the reduction of the numbers of emperor penguins. From recent research, scientists came to a consensus agreement that these species of penguins might be overly sensitive to the increase of the ocean temperature.

And evidently, a loss of ice will directly mean a decline in the number of emperor penguins. Not that alone, they will be liable to attacks by predators, their large area of habitation and for breeding will become smaller and surviving becomes difficult.

5. ***How Amphibians Are Fairing.*** Toads, newts, frogs, and Caecilians which are amphibians are also subject to climate change too; they are not excluded. It is genuinely hurting that among vertebrates, the negative impact of climate change affects these sets of amphibians the most.

One major thing about amphibians is that when it comes to being sensitive, they are highly sensitive. Any slight alteration in their habitat results into an imbalance. If there occurs a change, even though little in the amount of rainfall and temperature, they would still be affected.

6. ***How unusual rainfall threatens Orangutans***. Bornean and Sumatran, which are two species of Orangutans are also severely affected by climate change.

One, oil palm producers drives them off their habitat thus losing their habitat. In addition to human-made influence, when there are inconsistencies from the rain, it affects fruiting, making it tedious for Orangutans to feed.

A close example of these terrible events is what happened in 2007, where rain didn't fall at the right time, drought sets in, forests were so dry and an uncontrolled fire from an unknown location surges and destroyed the forest killing over 1000 Orangutans while they were in their forest habitat.

If not controlled, this situation isn't halting anytime soon. In fact, scientists have predicted that this occurrence will be on the high side.

7. *Clownfish Are Being Drifted Away by Storm Intensity and Coral Bleaching*. With the aid of chemical signal, coral reef conveniently locates their way to the coral reef.

But, the effect of climate change brings about the difficulty in locating their habitat. When the seawater becomes more toxic as a result of climate change, locating anemones would be delicate. If farther from the chemical for a very long time, they would likely lose their immunity to its position.

Another important fact is that, at a very high temperature, something related to climate change, reproducing is a fairy-tale. The egg can be damaged thus hindering the production of young ones.

Now that you've gained insight into how climate change affects the animal. Animal migration is an important aspect to talk about because for proper function of the ecosystems. And interestingly, one has to know how climate change affects animals' migration pattern, or they have immunity regarding that. Well, if they do, then how does it happen? The next sub-heading will treat that.

**Impact of Climate Change on Animal Migration**

Genuinely speaking, at any slight alteration in biotic and abiotic cues caused by climate change, animal migration is susceptible to disruption. How it does it is by altering it systematically.

A long time ago, Scientists predicted that species migrate as the climate condition changes too. But the only factor limiting this prediction is that they aren't aware that it would come so rapid. And that is precisely what happened. The recent research indicates that a tally of more than 3500 species found around the globe shows that nearly half of the species are currently on the move.

For example, species on the land are migrating on an average of 10 miles per 10 years. In sharp contrast, marine species are moving just so rapid, in fact, more than four times faster than land species' speed. Other species are even moving more quicker and swifter. A noble Scientist at the Plymouth University, Camille Parmesan said that Atlantic cod in the United Kingdom Migrated More than 12o miles just in 10 years. Quite disturbing, right?

Further, the timing of biological cycles is moving due to the warming that results from climate change. Well, sadly where the difference is going to halt is no clear and direct

because species amidst an ecosystem make their movement in two category - space and time! Yes, the change or shifting as some prefers it don't come in the same area, and the signals they respond to is never the same.

For some, their adaptation is based on alteration on temperature, while for some, modification comes from influences from sunlight, and precipitation. All around the globe too, there are appearing of new hybrid species, namely trout, toads, bears, sharks, and butterflies. These are just a few of the documented species that have been randomly merged due to climate change.

Moreover, the untangling of some ecological relationships is what is threatening some other types of species. Take for examples, a shorebird

41

that travels from the tropics down to the Arctic every spring just for it to have a source of sustenance - feeding on insects. Why? It has recently experimented that Arctic snows are currently subjected to melting, and consistently insects hatch weekly before the arrival of the bed although there is even little food for the shorebird to feed on.

Likewise, mortality of some species is on the increase. Young caribou, for example in West Greenland, are dying because of the difficulty to feed. The plants that their mothers feed on in the calving season are not sufficient. Also, in Japan, Corydalis ambigua is flowering rapidly before the arrival of bumblebees for pollination. This leads to the production of little seeds. In the meantime, bumblebees worldwide are being pushed out of the southern region due to increased temperature.

David Inouye, who is an emeritus professor with the great citadel, University of Maryland, College park asserts that anyone who creates time to spend outdoor to take a closer look to watch birds, hunt animals or fisherman, they would realize that timing, as well as migrations, are drastically changing.

More to the point, birds that are migrating are responding to the impacts of climate change by arriving earlier at their new habitat before temperature rises. This point was fully substantiated at the University of Edinburgh where more than a hundred birds were examined. The result gotten shows that birds are getting to their summer breeding grounds a day earlier per degree of rise in global temperature.

For birds, two of the most vital reasons why they migrate is due to the search for food and inconsistencies in the seasonal temperature. Impressively, the bird's time must be accurate, because a delay could cost them a nice place for nesting and getting food. This would adversely affect their reproduction and chances of survival would glaringly impact their survival.

More research has shown the types of species that would travel either long distances or short distances. They include Pied flycatcher and swallow and pied wagtail, respectively. As experimented, a swallow is migrating, for example can travel more than 200 miles in just a day at a maximum speed of 35mph.

Recently, it was also predicted that more than 520 species had been fully and adequately documented in San Diego. Nevertheless, the number is expected to decline. According to Phil Unitt, who works at San Diego Natural History Museum, there is the likelihood that climate change hits them in the years to come. Unitt even insisted that each species will be complex on his own.

Unitt even further explained that migration of bird is highly influenced and would be halted in the face of temperature, so they can keep an eye on possessing a new habitat that is cooler and a bit wetter.

Another reputable source of information, The National Audubon Society predicted that more than half of North America's bird species would be compelled to get a new habitat for themselves.

More points from Unitt even made it clear that birds that wouldn't adapt to the altering climate change will miss the height of food surplus as soon as they arrive at their reproductive grounds. So, if after getting to a location, they discovered that the insects have a reduced number compared to in the past, they wouldn't nest. Then hat next. They have to migrate further.

We realize that climate change influences other aspects like extinction. Because what happens after several days or month of seeking for a survival. Is it possible to get back to the origin? Next point talks more on if climate change can lead to extinction. Can we take a few trips to find out?

## Can Climate Change Lead to The Extinction of And Animals?

If you want the answer so quick and straightforward, the answer is, yes! But if you are in for more convincing points as to how this can happen. I advise you to read on.

43

First and foremost, anthropogenic climate change is highly speculated to be a critical cause of species extinctions, in the next century. But you could desire an explicit explanation on what causes these extinctions.

Take for example, could it be only restricted to physiological tolerance and extremely high temperature. Could it also be the result of altered biotic interactions or other several factors? Exercise patience, we will certainly get an answer to these questions.

Fact is, climate change is a heinous threat to all species and protecting species from its detrimental effect would be challenging to do. Also, climate change could have significant interactions with several anthropogenic impacts. For modern scientist today, having a large and all-solution faces biologist.

Well, all animals possess a temperature range, that is, a particular temperature that fits in their survival, and when it goes beyond that, suffering knocks, especially, death!

Even though to a reasonable length, animals can migrate towards to ascertain a more comfortable temperature zone for their survival, as there becomes a more noticeable change in the temperature globally. Take a closer look at mosquitoes and fish. Fish for example, as a result of climate change, they shift farther from their initial geographic locations. Mosquitoes can transfer dengue and malaria farther from their equator as well.

There are limitations to the extent to which they can move. For example, some species can't go either north or south because they have come across physical limits which

could be running into humans and agriculture which will lead them into more threat to their life, inability to get a befitting habitat for survival.

As the year passes by, typical climate observers would note extreme weather condition is becoming to hit the globe harder. Look intently at what's happening in the Great Barrier Reef. The coral bleaching events make coral reefs growth becomes stunted and slow — this limited migration into the southward.

In the marine habitats, heat waves as a result of climate change have killed some seagrass. And these aforementioned, corals, sea-grasses serve as shelter and food for numerous species that finds it difficult to live somewhere else.

Think about the alteration in rainfall, sea level rise, acidity, the evaporation, and storm frequency. They will undoubtedly amount to a change in the environment, in fact leading to a more intolerable condition. Happily, some species would be able to adapt gradually; it might even lead to a new way of functioning with the ecosystems. But for some, the reverse is the case, and it will thus resort into extinction.

Anthropogenic changes are also modifying physiological tolerances. And coming from different angle extinction could be reached from diversities of ways. When there is a decrease in precipitation, more death could be recorded. Since there will exist water stress and another form of local extinction right for terrestrial species, and the misplacement of habitat.

However, some species would be favored by an alteration in temperature while some wouldn't, they would come glowing and shining if the change is in the precipitation.

Furthermore, other several abiotic factors can also lead to animal extinction. In some cases, fire frequency, a result of climate change, can lead to destruction. Likewise, the rising sea levels and melting of the ice cap are sufficient to eliminate coastal habitat and would go a long way to adjust the salinity of fresh water.

Biotic factor from climate change, when traced, could also lead to the extinction of species. These may be classified into three. The first one which is the negative impact on beneficial species means that climate change will result in the extinction of a particular species when there is a reduction in the size of the species it depends on.

Second, the positive impacts on dangerous species. Climate change could lead to the extinction via positive effects of species that possess ill relationships with a focal species which cuts across competitors, and pathogens.

Thirdly, this involved non-permanent mismatch among interacting species. Climate change may result in an incompatible match of two species. But that form of matching is only short-lived.

At the point, you might ask: has it ever happened or is it happening presently? This question is highly relevant; it goes a long way to validate all I have been explaining at the onset of this subheading. Even though some extinctions should not be traced down climate change, yet, a few species all over the world that have gone extinction can be determined down to climate change. Let me highlight a few examples.

Out of about 864 species extinctions examined by IUCN (International Union for Conservation of Nature) that have occurred in recent times, only 20 of these species comes from climate change. Well, the claims are tenable and valid.

Conclusively, climate change is now identified as a significant problem to global biodiversity, and it is held responsible too for the extinction of some species. Over the years, the changes in climate are expected to be rapid, this, in turn, will rapidly increase the rate at which species will go extinct, say in a century to come.

Remember, while discussing how climate change affect animals while explaining I made mention of some animals, though, it wasn't exhaustive. The point I needed to create your understanding was for you to see it yourself. But there are still many species that are being affected by climate change; this is more on how those species are being affected. Read on to familiarize yourself the more with this.

## How Fifteen Animal Species Are Affected by Climate Change

From different locations and areas where animals are present, animals are being affected by the constant changing of climate. The climate patterns that change warrants the need for animals to align themselves

46

with the change, the continued increase in the greenhouse emissions has made animals lost their habitat, and lastly, animal breeding has been negatively impacted just for survival. Either being directly affected by an increase in temperature or inability to get food source, the animal is facing the imbalance of the system.

But think about this, if these animals aren't able to migrate to a more safe and reliable habit, what becomes of them? Extinction, apparently, right? Your guess is as good as mine.

Learn further about how the ten species I will be mentioning will reveal what animals are facing, and also, I will be sure to be exhaustive! Although, the animals that will gain my mention aren't just the only animals affected by climate change. But, be rest assured that this list will be extensive enough.

1. *Asian Elephants*. They are gentle giants. They have high sensitivity. More reason any alteration in their temperature, they are being affected. The increase in temperature leads to regular consumption of a large quantity of fresh water daily. In most cases, getting that large amount of water can be a grim task, if they can't get water, as a result of drought, they will leave for the search of water.

2.*Giant Panda Bears*. If this isn't your first time of reading on panda bears, you'd be familiar with their meal, bamboo. Bamboos serve more than 85% of your consumption still. This species feed exclusively on bamboo. Sadly, climate change is presently wiping off the abundance of bamboo off their natural habitat. Bamboo doesn't only provide food for this type of bear; it serves as a habitat for them to thrive; a shelter to live in. Climate change isn't solely responsible this time. Agriculture, construction of magnificence infrastructure are human activities that pose a threat.

3. *Cheetahs.* Even though cheetah is recognized to be one of the world's land fastest animal, it is still not immune to this ruthless impact

of climate change. Unfortunately, the speed isn't helping in this regard. But how they are being affected is indeed amusing.

You know that cheetahs have prey, if due to climatic change they are affected, cheetahs too would, because, at the very least, they have to change their diet. Apart from the change in diet, climate change is influencing their ability to reproduce. From male cheetahs, investigations have shown that their sperm count has gone down, something ten times lower than any house cat.

4. *Orange-spotted Filefish.* This fish's habitat is found comfortably among coral reef habitats; if you've been reading from the beginning, you would be sure of where we are driving at. Coral reefs are declining as a result of climate change, then what will become of other species that seek dwellings in them?

Additionally, orange-spotted filefish are also sensitive, and most especially to warm water. In the year 1988, in Japan, when ocean temperature becomes warmer, this animal went extinct. And this aftermath was just the result of a change in the ocean temperature.

5.*North Atlantic Cod.* Since time immemorial, fishing had been a significant occupation in many parts of the world. However, instead of having a reduction, the fish population is returning to its usual stat. But there is an exemption. In the northeastern coast of North America, the community of fishes being captured failed to recover.

Research from scientists shows that what would have made that happened would be nothing less than a change in the ocean current at the regular influx of cold Arctic waters which is brought by climate change. And if not halted all other species in other regions could be placed under the same fate too.

6. *Golden Toad.* Sadly, this species has gone extinct. This is just a few among the small numbers of species that have been thrown out of life by climate change. Scholes and Portner, renowned scientists, agreed that there is medium confidence that climate change results into the extinction. Before extinction, it was last seen in 1989; they stay in

mountaintop cloud forests. But ask me what has happened to the cloud forest? It has gone off due to the drought that came about because of climate change. So, what would become of the told seeking refuge under it? Same fate!

7.*Moose*. It is very likely that this species of animal would have to migrate farther north. This is due to the devastating impact brought upon by climate change. Take, for example, booming parasite populations and the warmer temperature is a threat to this cold-friendly species.

Well, when winter becomes milder, and there occurs little or minute snow, and this would lead to winter tick. Progressively, in thousands, this parasite can gather comfortably on a moose. Before you know, they've weakened moose immune species which sadly would lead to death.

8. *Snowshoe Hares*. Dishearteningly, beautiful snowshoe hares are being affected by climate change. Predators are one of the reasons these hares have migrated to turn white to blend accurately with the snow. However, snow in some areas melts sooner than when the snowshoe hare gets there and adapting becomes a problem since they would be exposed to a severe condition, snow-less landscapes.

As the time passes by, this might sadly lead to the decline of the hare's populations, and as expected when it happens, it will lead to other species suffering this same menace as well, since snow hares are a beautiful animal that plays a significant role in the forest ecosystem.

9.*Puffins*. We all know how beautiful, elegantly- looking, puffins are. These look identical to miniature penguins. Not long, research has shown that this species is also experiencing difficulty in reaching a destination where food could be found. Their major meal, herring, and hake are difficult for them to get at the Gulf of Maine.

Also, as the sea warms, the fish are gradually heading into deeper waters, then for puffin to feed on them becomes highly tricky. Though the big puffins are profoundly helping at least by supplying their young ones, they aren't able to eat, because they are large. So, when not able to eat, starvation knocks and thus dying becomes imminent.

49

10. ***Piping Plovers.*** What threatens these species are very much in number. For example, continual human use of the beaches where piping plovers use as a habitat affects their survival. Rising sea levels and high coastal development are not friendly at all. It displaces them as a species and makes feeding highly tricky for them.

11. ***Salmon***. Salmon species and its population are under severe attack. Salmon's survival is dependent on the availability of cold and fast flowing streams, and rivers. But when these situations come otherwise, the condition leads to a threat to their survival.

Apart from the havoc a warmer temperature would bring to salmon, it pushes salmon's parasite. We should expect nothing than a reduction in the population of salmon. And more expansively, it will alter commercial and the fishing industries in the years to come.

12.***American Pikas***. This animal habitat needs to be cool since that is the only favorable climate to its survival. But recently, a geological survey in the U.S. came up with research that reveals that this species is disappearing from various locations. In some areas, some other species migrating to a higher elevation are becoming a usual occurrence. This is to ensure that they aren't exposed to a warmer temperature. Sadly, Pikas can't do that. Since they are heavily glued to rocky-talus habitat and this type of habitat is patchily dispersed and not even abundant. In the meantime, the temperature keeps rising with a few or no options; they die.

13. ***Alaskan Caribou.*** One of their enjoyed endeavors is to search for a meal! For that reason, migrating becomes a part of their lifestyle. This might make it seem to you that there exists little problem. But increase temperature leads to wildfires which happens for a very long time, and in turn, it will alter Caribou's habitat and winter food sources.

And sadly, these species will be susceptible to farmers that feed on them for nutritional values. Also, they use transcends to economic and cultural purposes.

14.*Koala.* Climate change isn't also friendly on Koala. Research has revealed that in 100years to come, this iconic animal is set for extinction. For Koalas, their food is highly restricted; they feed on eucalyptus leaves. But when the level of carbon dioxide is being increased, the health benefit to be gained from the leaves becomes something else, some of the low nutritional value. This goes a broader range in leading to Koala's starvation and malnutrition.

Also, the consistent drought would influence bush burning, and this unarguably will destroy millions of koala's species, in fact destroying their means of sustenance. And for those that will be alive, they would be compelled to get down off trees and search for water to drink, thus migrating becoming unavoidable, as they become exposed to predators.

15.*Monarch Butterfly*. I don't want any ill to happen to this intelligent creature. With no order, the monarch can travel a long distance and still locate its origin. One of the most impressive migration is the movement from North America to southern America. Just like some other butterflies, Monarch is very sensitive to both climate and weather alteration. As it stands, Monarch is susceptible to intense weather events. Additionally, Monarch's meal is unique and limited. As this charismatic bird feeds on milkweed alone, the warmer the climate becomes, the ability to feed on important food becomes more difficult.

Did you enjoy reading this enlightenment? I promised you that it would be exhaustive, was it note? We should both have a feeling of care and concern. As a result of this, I have decided to let you see, how you can extend a loving hand of attention to these species, all of them mentioned and those not in the list. No one is excluded; it is what we can all do. The next paragraph will be explicit on that subject.

## Tips to Help Adopt Environmentally-Friendly Lifestyle

Take a moment and ponder over the animals I mentioned- the cute, pretty and little ones. Imagine waking up one day and reading the news that they are nowhere to be found? Would it be good news? It's nothing close to an excellent report. That is why we should strive, assiduously to contribute our quota in helping the ecosystem, see how we can live a life that becomes more friendly to the environment and most especially, these animals that are under attack.

The International Union for Conservation of Nature reveals a bothering list that says that over 5,000 species are being affected this includes subspecies of animals. It didn't stop there; they still explained that close to 20,000 species are also vulnerable to the attack from climate change.

Hunting, poaching are leading reasons why these animals are often being endangered. Pangolin is a closed species that is wrestling the impact of climate change as a result of human influence. These species meat is edible, and additionally, they are being used as traditional medicine. And as this continues, they continue to be severely endangered. And as a result, the population is reducing drastically.

Sadly, the trafficking of these particular species hasn't stopped.

Both people and animals use this planet earth. Being an animal lover, learning to know how to reduce the negative impact of climate change is essential. Even if you are nowhere close to being an animal lover, you still have to care for the health of the earth - both man and animal.

Over the years, smart individuals have been doing fantastic and thrilling things have been working hard to get off this lousy impact. Though new inventions are coming each day, and these make gases filled in the earth and make our planet earth warmer which leads to the melting of the sea ice and the rising of the sea levels. The ways to adopt this and be more friendly with the animals is by taking these following tips.

1. *Adopt a Meatless Meal:* You can schedule this to be either one day or two per week. In the agricultural sector, like meat and dairy discharge more greenhouse gases. And sadly, this is even higher than what the world's transportation also releases. This thus shows that the process of producing beef, lamb and cheese amount one of the most massive and most significant amounts of greenhouse gas emissions.

Now, if an individual can cut on the consumption of meat and beef, no doubt, there will be a drastic reduction in the amount of greenhouse gases discharge. But how can you do that? It is not difficult. Some guides would help you to come up with a healthy and enjoyable alternative. That even you will be surprised that you can do it.

There are incredible, realistic ways to consume less meat. You may decide to eat some of the nutritious vegetarian meals or making sure that the amount of meat in you eat in a meal is lessened.

I'll highlight five ways you can achieve these.

- *Go meat-free for one day per week-* This pattern will let you gain 15% of your meat reduction, multiplied by the whole population, amazing not so? Great!
- Always Eat More protein as a Rich Substitute. Enough protein meals will help you become more fuller for a long time, thus reducing your quest to get a meal which might tempt you to take more meat. Daily consumption of 0.8 grams of protein by a kilogram of body weight is highly efficient.
- Do a new experiment with vegetables and grains. This adds new flavors and more textures. It discourages seeing your meal as a boring dinner.
- Substitute Your Favorite Food for a meat-free version. Mushroom sausage rolls, if loved by you would undoubtedly be a better alternative to sausage rolls - made with meat.
- Go for Unprocessed Snacks. You can achieve maximum nutrition that brings rich satisfaction even when you don't have meat at all.

2. Discourage Deforestation in a larger Scale. Most animals whose habitat regardless of the climate change they are presently facing are still being displaced. These are becoming more alarming. Regular felling of trees are putting some species homeless; they have no magnificent abode to call their home anymore.

Also, there exist some grassland that today they've been diverted into something else. They have been used in building estate. To make some designs, most ponds water are being drained out. If afforestation is more encouraged, most of this displaced animal will find that way back into their home.

The government has a part of executing too. Programs that encourage preservation of new species like new improved laws about the felling of trees, areas that should never be infringed to avoid penalties. If these provisions are made on the ground, it would have been of tremendous help to the animals.

3. Do Away with Disposable Cups. Sadly, disposable cups are heaping a significant threat to the life of animals worldwide. Take, for example; statistics show that workers are using about 500 disposable cups every year in the American office. These cups do not recycle fully, even in the next five centuries, all these would still be retained on the land.

For a fact, plastics that aren't being disposed into the ocean is still hazardous to animals. And their impact is just identical to those experienced in the marine habitat. One of the problems to be encountered is accidental consumption, which apparently could be a violent end.

For plastic beverages, Americans alone, in each hour, disposes of about 2.5 million synthetic drinks.

One of the ways to solve this problem is to adopt recycling. But how about reusing? That is indeed the best and reasonable approach!

However, there is numerous alternatives to the use of disposable cups. Think about the advantages that come from the use of this alternative. There will be less waste overall, less energy that increases carbon-dioxide, fewer spending. At work, always go with your cup. This will reduce the tampering with natural resources that animals depend on for survival.

3. Always Use Bulbs with Energy Star Label. Investigations show that bulbs with energy star label have the potential of reducing the greenhouse gas discharge that influences global warming.

Carbon-dioxide is responsible for the more significant part of the airborne pollution, and it is termed "greenhouse gas." When there is a discharge of carbon dioxide into the atmosphere even though little, it will extract warmth's and retain artificial heat in the atmosphere. When more fuels are being burned to generate energy, the extra carbon waste is not healthy; it goes beyond the natural occurrence. And expansively, it impacts life and land. Thus, it will lead to an increase in the rising temperature, drought; it would lead to higher sea levels, acid rain and irregular weather pattern and more occurrence of a natural disaster.

So now, check your bulb and check if they are energy savers. If they are not, then replace them. It is realistic to cut back on energy consumption as it limits the amount of energy needed for power plants to generate, which indirectly reduces the level of fossils that are being burned regularly.

Apart from helping the environment, you are supporting the animals. How? It saves the ecosystem and animals. Scientists say that human-impact is one of the reasons that biodiversity are vanishing so rapidly. And it's even a thousand more than the average rate.

Oil spills that take place each time fossil fuels are being transported are harmful and toxic to marine life and cause an imbalance in the ocean. How about how it benefits your purse? As estimated, you will save $70 per year on energy bills. Additionally, the lifespan is way higher and more significant than the non-energy saver, about 10 to 50 times longer.

Starting from now, if you have not been doing that, anytime you intend purchasing an electrical appliance, be sure to buy the one that has Energy Star label.

4. Speak Out, Make Contributions. Staying at the comfort of our home isn't sufficient to become more environment-friendly. Think about what

compelled me to go this length to educating the public about climate change and the impact. I'm making my voice heard; you too can do.

It is essential you make representative of legislative seat aware of the menace threatening animal which when not curb could lead to unprecedented extinction.

Look for environmental agencies around, inform them that you support their moves. And then offer to see what practical approaches that have been used in fighting ecological problems for decades. For more in-depth check, inquire if there is a benefit or sanctions for companies who switch to a more sustainable energy adoption, and those who fail to and have been stiff-necked thereby increasing the susceptibility of animals to climate change.

Another pattern of consulting a representative or a person of high authority could also be to forward a formal letter. It is often realistic when an elected leader is aware that the masses aren't comfortable with the destruction of this beautiful planet.

After all, some fundamental laws and regulations are in line with environmental sanitation. These laws are in place to protect what animals drink, eat and the air they breathe. Thus, more unitedly, if elites could stand up regionally and internationally to speak out, those in positions of authorities will indeed honor that, do something about it and then will restrain more damage that looms in the future.

5. Drive Less. Driving habits hurt the health of animals. Driving undoubtedly pollute the environment. And threatens the habitats of most animals. You can reduce the impact of climate change by limiting how you use your car if you have a personal vehicle. Below, I will be explaining five realistic ways of driving less and enjoying the peace that comes from knowing that you aren't rendering animals extinct.

- Use Bicycles. Most especially when you leave close to your working place, then you have an excellent opportunity to carry this out. Riding to work with a bicycle helps you in getting great and fresh air. Additionally, it makes you get your body fit. However, it is not mandatory you keep riding to work each time. But it is something you can do either once in a week or twice a week. That little adjustments, if adopted by plenty people will have significant improvement. Even though your friendliness to the ecosystem is what is motivating you to do this, be reminded of these benefits - fresh air and staying fit!

- Share with Others. It is possible that you aren't the only person driving from your neighborhood. You can share with folks by teaming up with them, instead of having five cars on the traffic, it would be five people in the car!

That's an excellent save. You will save on gas and stress. Thus, every day, you'd not have to drive. Additionally, there are some specific times you'd desire to do some work or read while heading to work, but when you are behind the wheel, it impossible, unless you are just set for a disaster.

To enjoy the liberty of doing other works and probably reading, hook up on sharing, it will be of tremendous help. The only problem that could hinder this process is identifying who you'd want to share with. To solve that, numerous applications have been developed to solve that problem. These apps will match you with nearby commuters.

Organize Some Road Trips. Be reminded that this point isn't in any way advocating that you should neglect your car entirely. Don't forget that our primary goal is to do all you can to save the animal and while you do that, you can enjoy more personal benefits. During weekends, instead of going out with cars, you can take your family out for hiking. This conserves the fuels to be burned by motorcycles.

Use Public Transit. Most cities have affordable public transport. There are developed cities whereby you can accurately predict the arrival time and more offers. Applications like Transit and Quickly are efficient in making this move. Nevertheless, if you are indeed late either for a meeting or an appointment, it is better to make use of your car. But it isn't a bad idea to wake up early so you can get the bus in the early hours of the day.

Review Your Insurance. Do you know there exist insurance dubbed "pay-per-mile" car insurance? Yes, definitely! Now that you have agreed to adopt this new pattern it is a nice move to review your coverage. This will make you save more money in metro-mile.

Interestingly about 65% of U.S are driving 200 miles a week. I'm sure you are getting the trend. Join these intelligent folks to make a better change to our society.

Conclusively, everyone should make its goal to keep climate change under control.

**Chapter Three**

# Climate Change and Water

## Overview

Water, a vital resource that both the ecosystem and the society depends upon is never to be taken for granted. Unfortunately, the satisfaction of water resources isn't only limited to any water we see; it has to be clean, safe, reliable for drinking.

Also, water is the primary medium by which the overwhelming impact of climate change is being felt. Yes, records show that water availability is coming to be less and less predictable; this includes many regions, increasing the contaminate water sources, sanitation procedure including erecting the facilities to be used, and destruction of water points.

From differing regions, droughts are immensely hitting water availability, and it has an impact on peoples' health and their productivity. While it is reliable that everyone has access to sustainable water and clean water, it is relevant to be able to identify the problem, though picking up solutions would make much sense to every sane person.

Other areas of need for water resources like agriculture, energy, manufacturing, navigation, recreation, and the product has to be suitable for the intended usage. Sadly, in meeting the global demand for this, unprecedented pressure has been mounted on water, and these pressures are likely to be exacerbated by climate change.

Right now, in some regions, most regions, climate change could be responsible for an increase in water demand and limiting the supplies of water. You will agree with me that this isn't a balance. This imbalance would no doubt set a challenge ahead of water managers to meet the demands of many communities, manufacturers, a sensitive ecosystem, energy producers, and farmers.

In sharp contrast, having a supply of less water will never be a big deal, but they have to wrestle an increase; flooding, runoff or increase in sea level rise are significant challenges they would have to overcome. The result of these events would impact the quality of water, and disrupt the infrastructure used in the transporting and delivery of water.

To solve the problem of climate change, it is essential that you build climate change resilience via water management and ecosystems. As you read in this chapter, always bear these:

Climate resilience is being reinforced via good ecosystem services that are resting on the accurate-functioning river basins.

Climate change leads to direct aftermath conflict and water security.

Climate change presents itself mainly via changes in the water cycle. Then, as climate changes, melting glaciers, sea-level rise, droughts, intensify storms, floods and then do not leave behind unfortunate consequences.

An effective country-driven climate change adaptation technique must at all cost reflect the vitality of water management in limiting vulnerability and constructing climate resilience.

If climate change adaptation would be applied to acquire Sustainable Development Goals, building climate resilience is paramount.

This real issue is that water which serves as the fragile balance that exists between precipitation and evaporation is the main cycle via climate change is experienced. As at present, just 3% of the planet's water is freshwater, and in fact, two-thirds is being seen in both polar ice and glaciers. Worse yet, ensuring the safety of water for the global population has a higher rate that is highly demanding since it is set to get to about 10 billion by the end of 2050.

Knowing why it is vital is highly essential. Because currently, there exist a lot of stakes. In a 2015 verification of world crisis by The World Economic Forum, as to what disaster would have the most significant impact of damaging both economic and social implications with no country nor sector out of the forecast, Water crisis tops this list- It can't be more alarming than it is! If we have to live with the rapid changing of the climate, it would also translate to us battling with the impact on water. Regardless of the size, large or small. Also, it will have an expanse impact on how labile communities and economies are.

For a discussion of water security in this chapter, we will see how the direct impact has meant sad consequences on freshwater resources. Going by the current research that 4.8 billion people will be at risk of water stress before the end of 2050. The effort of water management is appreciated because it has assisted in driving trans-boundary cooperation, which entails one of the prominent aspects, water resilience. Also, it has expanded its coast by limiting the risk of a dispute between the countries that are being affected by the situation.

However, regardless of how dangerous and evil the consequences could be. There are varying ways it could be rendered. This chapter will address options that will make the community be better equipped in wrestling the disasters and any shock that will emanate from it. Solutions like a nature-based solution, where the use of mangroves, to prevent shorelines from running into storms, resist flooding plans to retain excess runoff, to disable lakes from storing large water supplies, will be discussed as you read on.

Climate resilience, which is another exciting part to help the strengthening of the healthy ecosystem will be explained too. We will see the four components, diversity, knowledge and learning, capital and innovation, and self-organization will not escape my mention.

Lastly, as you read, you will come to see how water plays an adorable role in how the world at large carries out mitigation, how it adapts to the effect. Although, there you will also see an integrated way of limiting the risk and would protect us from some of the grievous challenges.

To begin with, the water cycle and water demand are going to be the next sub-heading; how the water cycle is being impacted by climate change. Can't wait to start reading? Okay, let's journey down.

61

## Water Demand and Water Cycle

As previously briefed, the water cycle is a fragile balance of precipitation, evaporation and all the processes in between it. And with the advent of climate change that leads to warmer temperature increases the speed of vaporization of water back into the atmosphere. This hold to suggest that there will be more water in the atmosphere since the capacity of the atmosphere has been increased. This will mean the opposite thing for regions existing. Some will experience excess precipitation while for some, there will be drought.

The water cycle is an important phenomenon that enables water circulates via the planet's atmosphere and all available waterways which will reduce the quest of struggling with life, but instead makes stability and growth on earth possible and beautiful.

The changes in the rate of rainfall during storms provide the undeniable evidence that the water cycle is drastically changing. In the United States for example, for more than half a decade ago, the rate of precipitation has increased the number of a rainfall event.

Even in the Upper Great Plains, Midwest, and Northeast, they experience an increase. Additionally, warming temperature has also led to more precipitation to fall in the form of rain instead of dropping like snow. Moreover, the rising of the heat has led to storm starting to melt more rapidly in the first quarter of the year. And what does this result into? It impacts the timing of streamflow that occurs in rivers that their origin streams from the mountainous region.

With this temperature increase, the demand for water and animals becomes more demanding; it is needed for maintaining good health and for sustenance. Several economic activities require water. But sadly, the amount of water available may be reduced as the earth warms and the demand becomes more excessive.

Furthermore, science-proven often that climate change impacts every part of the ecosystem, and the water cycle is no exemption. Why? It is merely because every single step is highly reliant on temperature, and any slight change in one cuts across all others. As the world's temperature progressively increased at their rates in many thousands of years ago. This is majorly affecting water vapor concentrations, stream flow patterns, clouds, and precipitation pattern - all these are part of the water cycle.

But you might want to know that in what long ways has climate change impacted the water cycle. Water evaporates from the land and sea which will find its way back to earth in two forms, rain and snow. The rapid changes in the climates alter this process, the cycle, even further. The air temperature increases and leads to more and more evaporation of water into the air. As more vapor is being held in the atmosphere, warmer air would, therefore, lead to more rainstorms leading to flooding in coastal communities in the entire globe.

More to the point, this change results in different areas of experiences from stronger regions. Aside from the rain and drought explained earlier, there will be changes regarding dry air in some part, stronger storms in some areas.

To simplify your understanding about how climate change impacts water cycle, I'm going to breakdown the process into four stages.

Stage I: Increased in temperature will lead to more evaporation from both the sea and land into the atmosphere.

Stage II: This makes the air gets warmer, letting it hold more vapor, leading to more intense rainstorms.

Stage III: At the third stage, the increase rainstorms heighten the occurrence of flooding. Then, water runs into streams and rivers making it not do dampen soil the sufficient way.

Stage IV: All these combined, increase the risk of drought.

Although little has been said about how climate change influences water demand, there is still much to be discussed about the topic. Let's understand this from water demand management's perspective.

Water demand is understood as the demand for several services which include drinking of water, navigation, protection in case of storms, and irrigation. In a nutshell, the basic idea in water management is water security. The stress of a country as regards water demand is when the per capita water availability is below 1,000m3 per year based on actual runoff. And this figure entails the water needed for drinking, food production, and industry. Although, regrettably, the population in this category ranges from 1.4 billion to 2.1 billion.

But, water demand management itself can be explained and describes as any practical method either through the adoption of institutional, financial, economic or technical to accomplish these simple water demand task:

1. Limit the quantity or quality of water demanded to achieve a specific task

2. Alter the timing of use from peak to off-peak period.

3. Adjust the nature of the job so much water will not be used, and lower quality water will be used.

4. Ensuring that there will be enough water for the member of the public to use when the water is available in little supply.

5. Limit the quality and quantity of water significantly as it flows from the source through the use of disposal.

Currently, several tools and strategies are being employed in the enabling of water-use efficiency, equitable, sustainable practices and policies used although this would mean a restructuring in the way water is being used from varying angles especially in the areas of agriculture.

Water demand in a sense is an efficient way to meet up with the current challenge of water demand that leads to water scarcity and with continual impact in the climate, it will become more intensified. Water demand management also improves the resilience of society and how preparations are made in combating the problem.

Some of the water demand management is to ensure that campaigns for water economy at both industrial and household level, it includes economy in water use, pricing and some restrictions on users. It doesn't exclude some limits. For examples, some farmers might be restricted to a particular form or irrigation employed.

Summarily, water demand and water cycle are being severely affected by climate change, but the provision of water demand management would assist in curbing some of water demand's issue, thereby restoring the natural water cycle.

Since the demand for water is affected by climate change, water supply will undoubtedly suffer this same thing. Other analyses, which will be discussed further indicate that the alteration in the groundwater would be higher than the changes in the precipitation.

Take for instance, in areas where there exists annual rainfall that has a 20% increase due to climate change; there is the likelihood that at 40% the groundwater (water available in the ground) would increase again. Alternatively, the reduction in rainfall will have more impact on the underground. For example, a 20% decrease in precipitation will result in a 70% decrease in the amount of water recharging local aquifers. Will this not mean a devastating blow on in both arid and semi-arid regions? It will.

However, it should be noted, that some conditions will play their part, though complex they are essential factors. Take, for example; they include the type of soil, the type of vegetation, the duration and timing of rainfall events. Thereby there will be a need for a more comprehensive study in each location since no two places will have similar problems or conditions.

I am going by research made by many senior researchers and professors in the study of environmental engineering, water foundations. Experts like, Gene-Hua Crystal Ng, King Bhumibol, Dara Entekhabi, Bridget Scanlon, and others. The results they get was terrific, according to them.

They discovered that the changes in recharge might even be more significant than the changes in climate. Because the study discloses that for a change in the percentage of precipitation, there are more significant changes felt or experience in recharge rate. Also, the team noted another essential point. This point is the timing and duration of precipitation.

An instance seen is that there is more difference when it comes to the fall of much rainstorms or even smaller one, regardless of when they existed, either during summer or winter. Interestingly, precipitation changes often happen in an annual report, and what influences the recharge when the precipitation occurs, and how it can more be compared to growing seasons.

Well, while the group was presenting their result, they ensure that it is being offered as a possibility, yet they introduced what is aware of and what we know little about future climate and apparent changes. So, they conclude that for each prediction of climate change or alteration, a distribution of possible recharge values is unavoidable.

Therefore, even though there will be so much rainfall during plants growing, only little will find their way into the soil. Because the more significant part of the water will be absorbed by the vegetation and then returned into the atmosphere through transpiration while little will get its way into the aquifers, but one thing can be summarized from this investigation. Much rains could mean more water in the groundwater; less rain would mean lesser water in the aquifers.

For a comprehensive understanding of the knowledge of climate impact on the variability of water resources, there are about 10 facts you should know. Below, you can understand it better.

Presently, climate change is affecting the southeastern USA, particularly the increase in precipitation variability and air temperature. This has led to more occurring hydrologic extremes. Examples are high-intensity storms which include tropical cyclones, drought, and flooding.

2. Future climate warming would also lead to more water loss via the means called evapotranspiration as a result of increased evaporative

potential and shifting in the plant species. Any increase in the number of evapotranspiration will lead to nothing aside from groundwater recharge, total stream flow, and regional water supplies, and flow rate.

3. By 2050, there will be an increase in the amount of water stress due to the existence of hydrologic alteration happening as a result of climate change and increased water used by the major economic sectors, which include irrigation agriculture and power plants. Also, water supply stress is leaning to severity in the summer season since the average rainfall is not sufficient to meet the evaporative request of the atmosphere.

4. Also, the reduction and increase in the demand for water will likely lead to the pressure recorded on the reservoirs which will lead to a thicker and longer lasting reduction.

5. Soil erosion and potential runoff impact are increasing in some areas as a result of changes in rainfall that would lead to either erosivity or reduce vegetative cover protection.

6. Interestingly inland water temperature is forecast to increase as the air increases in temperature, which will affect cold-water fish habitat in the region of the Appalachians.

7. Also, in coastal freshwater systems, the salinity intrusion will increase in response to sea level rise and even lead to a decrease in the availability of freshwater inputs from the uplands due to climate change.

8. Also, any programs that will be used to increase water-use efficiency, used in ensuring the resuscitation of the water cycle, and an increase in water storage capacity should be developed to eradicate water supply issues.

9. The restoration of ecosystems which entails encouragement of afforestation would have a higher probability to mitigate or limit the negative impact of climate change on water quantity and quality.

10. Much is still needed to be learned about how future climate change and other factors, like human population growth, energy security,

upgrade in policies, and land use change will have an impact on both surface and groundwater availability.

Seeing that climate change is having an impact, a negative result at that on water supply, and the ecosystem. Even though the problem is critical, there are way out, from decreasing emissions to buying environmentally responsible products and expressing your support to other forms will be exclusively discussed at the end of this chapter.

But, In the meantime, let us consider how climate change impacts the ocean food chain. How this, in the long run, affects the ocean circulation patterns and how it alters the productivity of food chains.

## Climate Change Impact on Ocean Food Chains

Climate change isn't only warming the earth, but it is also altering the land. But how about the sea? It impacts it at a larger scale too; even though the additional heat emanating from the warming of the climate is near the surface of the ocean, and in the coming centuries, it will reach deep inside, the ocean circulation and ocean food chain are becoming less productive.

A recent study conducted from no less than five universities and laboratories examines how climate warming can have a severe impact on global fisheries and marine ecosystems. The idea of the study is to validate how continuous warming of the earth will affect the nutrients that act as a support to the tiny plankton, which serves as a meal for a fish in the ocean.

The result of the research shows that critical factors in the ocean will be impacted by climate change. Winds, water temperature, ocean circulation, sea ice cover will all be affected too. This damaging impact will drive the nutrients from the surface and reach down into the deep ocean. Hence the growth of plankton is shortened. Furthermore, if the marine ecosystem has fewer nutrients to feed on, it will lead to the reduction of global fish by 20% by the year 2300, and in the North Atlantic, 60%. In a broad scale, it leads to a significant reduction in the food source for millions of people.

The genesis of food production begins when the sun shines right on the ocean's surface. Then the microscopic organisms dubbed "phytoplankton," is the plants of the beaches grow with the help of the sunlight to grow. And down to about 330 feet, they can still improve. Apart from the sunlight, they depend on phosphorus, nitrogen which are rare in the surface waters.

This Phytoplankton are then eaten by tiny animals which in turn becomes food for small fishes, and then down to the top predators like shark and dolphins. But if some phytoplankton isn't consumed, they decompose in surface water and then discharge nutrients that will actively support the growth of the new phytoplankton, in turn, sink deeper into the ocean, then lead to food into the broad sea ecosystem. Phosphorus, carbon, nitrogen decompose too and fall into the deep also.

This short-highlighted process known as the biological pump, continues in dropping nutrients right from the surface down into the ocean. When the conditions are normal, without the alteration of climate change, winds and current will mix the sea and then takes the nutrients up to the surface of the sea. At the modification of the process, the cycle will not be completed, phytoplankton will run out of nutrients, and the entire food chain suffers wreck and havoc. Additionally, the function of the biological pumps isn't just to deposit nutrients all over the area of the earth's ocean, it also serves as a role for getting rid of carbon dioxide from the atmosphere, and when disrupted by climate change, it will lead to a more deadly result.

Regrettably, more carbon dioxide that is being made by human have been absorbed by the atmosphere and the oceans. This tends to cool off the earth back down; sea ice will get back to the polar oceans negatively affecting the growth and life of phytoplankton in the Antarctica region helping more upwelled nutrients to flow north just again into the lower latitude. And for ocean nutrients to get back its nutrients in the upper ocean, it will take more centuries. So bad!

Further, ocean resources being stressed have led to about 90% of the world's marine fisheries that are either being overfished or fished. And apart from the damage done to the sea life themselves. It will have an impact on a human shortly since it is estimated that in the coming future, say, in the year 2100, the world population is projected at 11 billion. Indeed, it will have a drastic impact on global food security. Sadly, even adopting aquaculture, which is, fertilizing the oceans to impel plankton growth will not also be sufficient to match up with the loss of nutrients to the deep sea that is caused by climate change.

Pondering on this havoc done to the sea life as at present, at least only a fewer fish are present in the ocean. One can imagine how deadly it will be shortly.

Now, let's see how climate change impacts water quality. Even though you've been getting a glimpse of it, there is more to that; you have to read more comprehensively about how this could is done.

## Water Quality

Water quality, a term used in describing physical, chemical, biological and radiological characteristics of water. It is a measure of the state of water relative to the requirements of either one or more biotic species or relating to the specific need or purpose. But, a little while back, water quality is suffering in areas where there exists an increase in the precipitation. Take an instance, in the Northeast and Midwest where there are many increases in the heavy rainfall, could lead to problems for the water infrastructure like water treatment plants, sewer systems.

Also, a substantial increase in the downpours can also bring about the increase in the higher rate of runoff down into the rivers and lakes. This can mean the washing off of more toxic substances, sediments, animal waste, pollutants, nutrients, and other materials into water supplies; they become unusable, unsafe and would require water treatment.

Also, freshwater resources in the coastal regions are faced with risks from the increase in the sea level. Just as the sea rises, saltwater migrates into freshwater areas. As a result of this unfortunate incident, many managers of water would or might prefer to seek to other regions for the dependent of clean water or increase the need for desalination for some coastal freshwater used as drinking water supply.

Moreover, if more fresh water is gotten rid of in rivers so that it will be suitable for human use, the tendency of saltwater moving farther upstream is very high. Also, drought can result in coastal water resources that will become more saline as the availability of fresh water supplies from rivers are limited. Furthermore, water infrastructure in the coastal regions leads to the rising sea levels and this impacts storm surges.

Remember I repeatedly mentioned coastal water supply. You might be wondering what coastal water supply is? I'll briefly explain it so that you can see how it impacts the Water quality.

### As it has been scientifically

investigated, it has been noted, that the quality of water supply in the island and coastal regions are at an unprecedented rate. The rising sea level and the occurrence of drought has the likelihood to increase the salinity of both glasses of water in the surface and ground via saltwater intrusion.

Take a closer look at this fitting real-life event. The freshwater Everglades presently recharge Florida's Biscayne aquifer, and it is the main water supply to the Florida Keys. When rising sea levels submerge low-lying areas of the Everglades, a few portions of the aquifer will become saline. The sea level will increase thus pushing salty water up the stream in coastal regions. To what effect? It threatens the provision of surface water.

Also, aquifers in New Jersey east of Philadelphia are often recharged by new portions of the Delaware River, and in any occurrence of drought, a severe one, it tends to be saline.

Freshwater though on some islands, most especially during small islands and atolls can be reduced since the supply relies solely on shallow aquifers which have been recharged by precipitation. These fresh waters lenses float on top of the saltwater while the rising sea declines the area above the sea level the lens stays. As a result, sea level rise can make

71

these shallow aquifers brackish through the flow of saltwater. and drought, in turn, reduces the availability of water from other sources, which will profoundly impact the stressing supply of water.

Now, since you've been armed with the knowledge of coastal water supply, I still want to discuss further on how climate changes impact water quality.

In Florida, last year, some species of animals, Slimy green and bad-oozing area were all over the beaches. Apart from the ugly sight of them and inconvenience from their smell, they are releasing toxins into the beaches that killed life in water, fishes, and shellfish. It has an impact on people; it got them sick.

Immediately, when the news becomes widespread, there was a declaration of the statement of emergency. And this, unfortunately, it led to economic damage. And if not checked, there is the tendency that many algal blooms will be found in the coasts and lakes as stated by the latest research. This shows explicitly that if the situation isn't checked, it can reduce to not the quantity - discussed earlier, but the quality.

Nitrogen, which is food for tiny algae are as a result of climate change sent into shore; then it feeds the algal blooms. Nitrogen traces its way into the waterways via a variety of sources. It could be as a result of the one used by farmers, the natural one produced by animals and humans from their dung, the emissions of fossil fuel. So, whenever it rains, the excess nitrogen is then washed right from the soil and air down inside lakes, to the groundwater and finally hitting the destination at sea.

The nitrogen blooms the algal, but when algae die, they tend to get to the bottom of the sea, get decayed and use up oxygen. Sadly, low oxygen is created, fish and shellfish will find it hard to keep alive; they will die. Apart from the impact on sea life, it also affects the supplies of drinking water that we all depend on.

It will be wise not to think that water quality is just a matter of local issue. Well, it is a beautiful thing to learn that governments are working on addressing this issue. They have improvised better working systems.

72

They have worked with farmers, educating them on how much fertilizer should be used. They have governed them on where the application should be made and when it should be made.

Also, limiting greenhouse gas emissions is also a realistic way of reducing nitrogen. Wastes should not be dumped into the environment, regardless of the type of garbage it is. There should be a way to reduce the rate at which improper dispose of waste is maintained. Although, there is much to be learned about greenhouse emissions into the ocean and see other ways it impacts to water, apart from the water quality which is just one.

## Greenhouse gas Emissions

Green gas emissions pose a threat to life, most especially, sea life. And then if it is not reduced, more lives will have to suffer this ill effect.

Sadly, even when all efforts are being driven into ensuring that climate change has little impact on life, there continues to be an aspect that plays a significant role in all life in the earth. For example, the increase in the green gas effect has been negatively impacting the atmosphere.

As defined, a green gas emission is any gaseous compound found in the atmosphere that can attract infrared radiation. As a result, they trap and hold heat in the atmosphere.

They accomplish this by increasing the heat in the atmosphere. If you'd have to track down the causes of the greenhouse effect, you need not go. Further, the reason is green gas emissions.

However, there is much we can do to limit the impact of green gas emission on the water to protect the water bodies. Impressively, the US EPA is working on a process on limiting the acidification of marine waters.

And if you are current about climate change, you will realize that just lately, scientists have risen to work on the ocean acidification that is becoming rampant and more and more alarming. Research has further shown that there is a connection between ocean acidification and atmospheric carbon dioxide levels. More studies have shown indeed that the ocean absorbs up to 20 million tons of Co2 each day from the atmosphere. Isn't that terrific?

This occurrence leads to an increase in the acidity that impairs marine's animal's ability to build and ensure maintenance of life in the ocean - shells and skeleton, and coral reef.

The continual help the agency worked on is ensuring the data gotten is substantial. They are sure of the possible changes in ocean acidity. It is no longer new that the government itself has admitted that ocean acidification is a threat.

They agree that strict actions must be adopted to ensure that clean water is protected. Immediate action should be done; else it will be catastrophic. Check below to see some of the best ways to solve green gas emission.

1. Reduce, Recycle and Reuse. When you buy products, ensure that the product is purchased with the intention to reduce waste. An experts result show that when you recycle half of your household waste in a year, you would have ended up saving more than 2000 pounds. Apply this rule to every household I am sure you would know what you will get.

2. Use Less Air Conditioning and Less heat. Just by adding insulation to walls and installing weather stripping around doors and windows, you can enjoy the potential of limiting the energy you require to heat or cool your home. Isn't that wise? And if you would have to use the heater, ensure that it is turned down while you are napping or off the house. And every time, always keep your temperature at minimal, moderate.

3. Use Less Hot Water. If you must use water heater, ensure that it is set within 120 degrees. And wrap it in an insulating material. For you to efficiently save hot water and more than 300 pounds of carbon dioxide yearly, invest in low-flow shower-heads. When you need to wash your clothes, wash them either in cold or warm water to help reduce the regular use of hot water, and the energy required to use it. The

experiment has shown that that adjustment alone is capable of saving at the very least 400 pounds of carbon dioxide annually in nearly all households.

4. Enroll for Report at Your Utility Company. Several utility companies offer free home energy audits. This is to enable consumers to checkmate their usage. They will be able to hand pick areas in their homes that would require energy efficient. Moreover, many utility companies present rebate programs that would allow the payment for the cost of energy-efficient upgrades.

5. Plant a Tree. How does your compound look like? Do you have a space to plant trees, then begin now! Get a shovel if you can, then start the work. But what impact does the tree have? Trees have the capacity of absorbing carbon dioxide and giving off oxygen. A single tree by experiment can absorb one ton of carbon dioxide in its lifetime. Even if you don't have the space to do that, look for people with the area and tell them the benefit of doing that, ensure that they are convinced and be reasonable when discussing with them.

6. Adopt The "Off" Switch. What is the off switch you might ask? It is the turning off of light each time you step out of your house. Saving electricity is also a remarkable way of reducing the impact of climate change. So, the bulb in your room, the sitting room should only be used when you are home.

Also, turn off the television, stereo, and other electrical appliances you aren't using. Each time you are using the water facility that has a connection with the electricity, always turn it on only when you will need it. Take for example, when brushing, do not leave the tap running, yet, turn it off until there is a need for you to rinse your teeth.

7. Teach Others to be Conservative. If you can adopt all those as mentioned earlier, you will be saving the planet at your capacity. But you need to teach others; encourage them. How can you do that? Share information consistently with people around you, your relatives, friends and if need be, your co-workers.

And it is good to tell public officers to establish policies that are effective for the environment.

In addition to green gas emission that impacts the water, sea life. Freshwater security is another issue that threatens water resources. How does climate change effect freshwater security? How can clean water be vulnerable and does it have scientific support? That leads us to the next subject.

## How Climate Change Will Impact Fresh Water Security

When there is access to fresh water supply, it improves the society, but the rising heat and shifting rainfall patterns, the reduced storage is having a significant impact on the availability of fresh water. States like the United States, Mediterranean, Middle East, and Mexico are not left out of the menace.

When we talk about fresh water, it is an important part that is essential to human society at large. Not merely for drinking, but for agriculture and several other activities. Climate change is gradually impacting the scarcity of fresh water in the future. For you to have a full grip of the problem of freshwater, you would need to understand first, how water is being distributed on the planet. And this is it:

98% of our water is salty, and just 2% is fresh. And only from 2%, 70% is snow and ice, while 30% and less than 0.005% are groundwater and surface water, respectively. At a global scale, climate change would have a significant impact on these proportions in a broader range, globally! One of them is that warming results into the melting of the polar ice into the sea, thus, converting fresh water into sea water, even though it has a little direct effect on water supply, we can't rid of the indirect impact.

Additionally, the effect of warming is to have an increase in the amount of water that the atmosphere can comfortably hold on to. They will lead to more rainfall, and more torrential rain each time the air cools. Though, you should be informed that more rain can provide fresh water, but when particular precipitation is heavier would rapidly and swiftly move water from the atmosphere back into the oceans. Thus, human ability to store and use this fresh water will be reduced.

Warmer air will directly translate to snowfall being replaced by rainfall, which will increase the evaporation rates. Another impact of the higher temperature is the melting of glaciers. In an average time, the level of supply of water to rivers and lakes will be increased. But as soon as the glaciers have melted, it will cease.

Nevertheless, in the sub-tropics, climate change can lead to reduced rainfall in the area already classified as dry regions. All in all, it will lead to the intensification of the water cycle (much has been said on this) which will mean extreme droughts and floods globally.

The effect of warming on freshwater availability is a crucial topic to talk about. In the recent IPCC technical report, they conclude that regardless of the global increase of rainfall, regions like the Mediterranean, Southern Africa, and other dry areas will be negatively impacted from reduced precipitation and higher evaporation. Thus, the conclusively, the result predicts that 1 billion people in the arid regions in the coming years will experience intense scarcity of water.

Notwithstanding, the rate at which this occurrence will take place is not known because of the current models adopted. Because in some regions different models are unable to predict whether some areas will be wetter or drier. Well, the direct impact of climate change shouldn't be the only reason why you as an individual must be keen about the future of freshwater security. Since the increase in the population will mean more demand for irrigation, and as the demand increase, it further leads to water pollution. Affluence could make some people still raise their daily water use. Even in areas of the rapidly developed economy, establishing more industries will mean more demand for water, and unfortunately, they come with zero water saving techniques and how to halt water pollution.

As a result of this, if there will be a keen concern for the freshwater scarcity, there should be an action that will make management of pollution and demand for water possible.

In fact, center for climate and life scientists place a focus on the future security of water resources, the access, and storage, with an enhanced understanding of how it works, they are being guided and this has helped to see some of the forces that are impacting water security at both local and international scale.

There are several ways of seeking a solution to the increase in the demand for water and ensuring that there are possible solutions to climate change impacts. One of it is redistributed freshwater over a more extended space and time. There should be a reservoir to be used in saving it, that is, storing it, there should be pipelines that will be used in transporting it. And more desalination to recover fresh water from the oceans.

Gladly, there are series of efforts put in place to increase water saving, reusing and recycling it. All countries should work hard to ensure that this is done. In the U.K., there are several investments in the educational sector and water-saving technology programmed by the government and water industry structure available.

As you have seen and read that climate change can have an impact on freshwater security. More is needed to be done; just like the UK government has done, there must be a continuous investment in education and further research should be made so that required knowledge would be gotten to develop skills and technology in fighting freshwater security.

Apart from the impact of climate change on fresh waters, the effects of climate change are increasingly being observed in the waters in the mountains. Do you know: Mountains stands as the origin for the earth's largest rivers?! Does it not worth learning? Are there even significant concerns? Learn more about this below and provide answers to these questions

## Climate Change and Waters in Mountains

Talking of mountains, they are one of the most sensitive regions to the rapid climate change experienced on the earth. Mountains also serve as a global water tower, and it naturally produces fresh water for populations around the world. This includes inside the hills themselves and to the communities downstream.

Notwithstanding, the energy gotten from mountain rivers and dam presents electricity for economic centers far from the mountains. This shows the role of mountains in the production of energy. Healthy and stable mountain ecosystem is such effective regulators of water catchments. The purpose is limiting sedimentation in reservoirs by disallowing erosion and also mitigating the risks of landslides and floods.

Mountains are highly fragile ecosystems. It has a complex topography - peaks, slopes, plateaus, steeps, and valleys all make their surface unstable. Might result in inappropriate human activities. Take, for instance, the continuous changing of climate itself, unsustainable land use practices, urban sprawling, deforestation of mountain forests and waste production are impacting the mountain ecosystems and watersheds.

Climate change, for one, posses so many threats to mountain areas. They are melting the glaciers rapidly and altering river flow regimes. This adversely influences the ecosystem, and it leads to flooding, natural disasters that impact, negatively the hydropower, and reducing the water available for irrigation. This problem does not only mean that we have to be working towards protecting the watershed; we must also engage the mountain communities and infuse them right into the system. And it must be in a way that is economical and culturally welcomed. Also, it should have the ability to strengthens their resilience.

More than 1.1 billion individuals around the world is finding it difficult to gain access to safe water. Also, some people who stay in developing countries where there is a very long existence of reliable water supply. The scarcity alters food production and leads progressively to an unstable society. But if more attention is placed to ensuring that the there is sustainable management of water in the mountains, that way the majority of the population would be able to have adequate fresh water and impressively serious consequences of water scarcity will be avoided, adverse effect on agriculture will not also be felt, most especially countries that are still developing.

No doubt, we can comfortably say that mountain system is vulnerable to effects of climate change. While it is true that one of the most significant impacts of climate change is felt in the polar region, the mountainous areas too are rapidly changing. Take an example, the rate at which climate change is occurring in the European Alps; it has become double than that of the average across the Northern Hemisphere. Plants are migrating towards the pole and are moving uphill too, just in a way that will make it easier for them to thrive.

We have said so much about how climate change impact water. From the water quality to water supply, demand, the freshwater security, the green gas emission and the just completed one, streams in the mountain. Now is the time we have to think about what you can do about climate change on water. Regardless of where the impact is being felt.

## What You Can Do About Climate Change on Water

Regardless of the impact, though brutal it might be, there are amazing solutions that have been projected. Everyone wants to be safe and secure both in their homes and communities. The value we place on clean water worth it.

Everyone can put efforts into limiting the havoc of climate change. Yes, we can help with our limitations and capabilities. Therefore, it is possible for us to change gradually until we achieve the primary goal, globally. It all boils down to practice. Also, you can include everyone in the steps to be discussed below. So, in this sub-topic, you will learn about ways to adopt from reducing car emissions, limiting energy expenditure in the home, limiting carbon footprint and many more.

1. Reducing Car Emissions. Reducing car emissions will save the water from becoming toxic for life in them, affecting their food chain and even to man. Processes to take include; leaving the car in the garage, use public transport, ensuring that your car tires are well inflated to the right and recommended pressure. Also, when driving, make it be slow or welcome the idea of car-pool with workmates.

2.Limit Carbon Footprint Each time you shop. At every shop, buy local and seasonal food produce. This will reduce the energy that will be used in transport and storage. You can also purchase items with minimalism in mind; that is, the packaging must be minimal. Also, if you buy new things, ensure that they are made right from sustainable, low-impact materials. Then finally, invest in quality second-hand material over the internet.

3. Recycle and Reuse. If you have so many rubbishes, recycle them. Also, make sure you compost vegetable scraps. In a more reasonable form, always detox your home. Dispose of any unwanted chemicals in a safe way rather than turning them into the sink or rubbish bin. Also, be creative in seeking and finding new ways to reuse an object.

4. Make Longer Term Choice. Making choices that will ensure that you are putting the longevity at heart is a quality way of being of help to the environment. If you stay far from your place of work, it is vital that you move closer to these places so that you can limit your walking distance, thus saving the time you will require to drive. Work changes can be made to ensure telecommute.

5. Be part of a Community Program. A community building network comprises different types of people with varying degree of experience that would influence how achieving a sustainable environment can be made. You can decide to begin a community garden that will be a source of education to yourself and others. Since the planting of trees absorbs carbon dioxide, you can converge people to help hold a community tree planting day. You can still get involved in your local council's activities that will assist in designing people and environment-friendly public spaces.

**Chapter Four**

# Impacts of Climate Change on Agriculture

## Introduction

Agriculture is a crucial sector in every country's economy; no state will willingly and deliberately take their concern off the tremendous help agriculture does to each of them! Aside from wrestling insufficient human resources, improper strategy, insufficient capital for effective executions of policies amongst others, is a troubling menace, climate change.

Admiringly, in the U.S. alone, crops, seafood, and livestock have a contribution to the whopping sum of more than $250 billion in strengthening the economy each year. Further, a combination of food-service and agriculture-related companies have made a tremendous impact, they've improved the gross domestic product, raising it to the peak of more than $700 billion. With these brief stats, who would argue the fact that agriculture needs keen attention by the government? Definitely no sane person would do!

Naturally, agriculture is excellent under moderate climate change. It is experimented and validated that when there is sufficient presence of carbon dioxide in the atmosphere, plants and crops germinate faster and grow well. But if the reverse is the case, that is, when floods, droughts and intense climate change occurs, it will lead to a reduction in yield, low-quality product and sadly limiting the availability of foods for consumption.

Well, for clarifications, there are so many incredible conditions that need to be satisfied for positive output on agriculture, for instance, the required water needed for the growth of plants must exist, the level of nutrients must be available, moisture for soil must be accurate; these are the conditions that need to be met, when the advent of climate change will leave farmers to battle with food safety.

Additionally, as I have explained vividly earlier, the warmer temperature will affect sea life, limiting their yield and the overall ecosystem. In like manner, the impact of climate change will extend to the total return of crops. Even apart from productivity, how farmers adopt the technology, many modern practices, and evolving ones will be negatively impacted.

Furthermore, if crop yield will be impacted negatively, there is no doubt that there will be an undeniable influence on food security. Yes, it will indeed be a challenge. And global food security is dependent on a sufficient level of access to food and adequate level of production. Should you need a comprehensive yet concise understanding of global food security, here we go:

Global Security is defined as the ability of the masses, at all times, have all right, economical, healthful and physical access to food totally with their improved diet and food likes and dislikes, hence a guarantee of healthy life will be certified!

It is disheartening that currently, one of the grandest barriers to food security is nothing other than food access. The need for food sufficiency is every day on the rise, the production of sufficient food is made to serve the current world population, yet, more than 8% of the world's population is being affected by impoverishment or undernourishment. The culprit isn't hard to identify.

Climate change, the culprit, is having a weighty impact on food security. It has led to an increase in the cost of food prices, leading to food insecurity in the future, and ultimately limiting the production of food. Thus, as this condition progresses, and worsens, food would become more expensive and scarcer. More so, the required level of water would be insufficient and inadequate for the production of food products.

Moreover, there will be considerable impact on land use. For, example, there will be a growing need for land use. It might lead to more dispute. How? Since only a few lands will be fertile and will guarantee large yield, a large number of people will be interested in having this crop-suitable land, but they will be insufficient, and to what end? Dispute!

Apart from the expected increase in the price, in more extreme cases, a sudden, unexpected increase in the amount of crop production will be experienced. And the fact for this assumption is found from the intense heat waves that hit countries like Kazakhstan, Russia, and other countries which affected their production of food. This unfortunate occurrence has led to more poor people on the rise, and with more conviction, it has revealed that climate change has the potential to influence food security.

More results have given more conviction on the impact of climate change on agriculture. Take, for example, the widespread agreement among Intergovernmental Panel for Climate Change (IPCC), indicates that climate change has occurred as far back as in the 1950s. The report didn't stop there; it goes further to explain that there is the tendency that there is an expected increase in the global mean surface air temperature as it will experience a rise of 0.4 heading to 2.6degree C, and precisely, this is going to take effect by the second half of our century.

Regardless of the terror increase in temperature can bring, drastic changes in the climate can not only be limited to this. It extends to changes in the precipitation patterns. More countries or areas are susceptible to flooding while for some, they are liable to drought. In cities, where sea rise is in its extreme, it may result in the loss, complete loss of agricultural land.

Sadly, a warmer climate will lead to more development of pests and diseases. It can impact the location of some pests, as migration due to climate change will influence them as well. These, in turn, might affect the animals in other regions that have not been affected by these diseases.

Well, there is much to be understood about the impact of climate change on agriculture, as the introductory aspect has given an overview of how agriculture is being impacted by climate change, I'll be elucidating further, more thoroughly on effects on crops, plants, livestock, fisheries, the global impacts, and how Agroecology could proffer the best solution both now and in the future, thus saving the globe from starvation.

For the following explanation and to assure a correct orderliness of points. The next article is bent on explaining fully, the relationship between agriculture and climate change.

## Relationship Between Agriculture and Climate Change

Going by the preceding paragraphs, you would have sensed an entwine relationship between agriculture and climate change. But how deep is the connection? You will unmistakably find that out as you read on.

Although the relationship between agriculture and climate change is dreadful, yet, it's worth learning. Before anything else, let's highlight the world population, how it is increasing, and the connection between agriculture and climate change.

It should not be new to you that agriculture is solely relying on weather and climate to cater for the resultant output - food for human sustenance. It is then, not astonishing that the impact of climate change is felt on agriculture.

Fact is, the increase in the population should also come into consideration if you would have a clearer and an undiluted understanding of the relationship between climate change and agriculture. Remember, the projected increase in population by 2050 is going to be about 11 billion. In sharp contrast, there is a forecast reduction in crop yields, and it is expected to be at 50% over the next decades due to the negative impact of climatic change.

In addition, agriculture has served hope for millions; it has become a spot for the deliverance of so many people. Through, agriculture, many have gained employment opportunities, thus, serving as a means of sustenance for so many people in the world today.

You can think about this: if there will be an increase in rapid changes of climate, it will have sternly impact on the sustenance of many families. It will so much have effect on the economy of the country, and indeed food production extensively. Sadly, among the African countries, Ethiopia is one of the largest states that is being rampaged by climate change. It has impacted their food security and produces. In the last decades, there exist an increase in the temperature in the region of Ethiopian. Per decade, it has a rise of 0.2-degree Celsius, whereas, in the last 50 decades, this type of increase hasn't occurred; it has remained stable!

Isn't this a high danger? Obviously. And when we sight a problem from afar, one of the reasonable approaches to take is to tackle it straight away. Going by the figure released by The State of Food Insecurity in the World, there is a figure of more than 700 million that have difficulty feeding.

So, if there is an alteration in the climate condition, it affects the availability of food, and the growing number of the population might not be sufficient for the available food for consumption.

Besides, the relationship between agriculture and climate change extends beyond the understanding of the increase in population. You would have seen that the brake or the stumbling block to meeting the required crops yield for the community is the climate change. Sadly, crop yield is making it more difficult to meet up. The decrease in the size of return we have is traced down to climate change.

But, surprisingly, agriculture itself which is being affected by climate change is also contributing to climate change? Shocking? It should if you are a newbie.

Agriculture leads to both direct and indirect emissions continually impacting climate change. For direct emissions, they emanate from any fertilized soils for agricultural purposes, while the indirect emissions are as a result of runoff, the fossils got from mechanization, more production of fertilizers, and even the repeated leaching of fertilizers.

Take, for instance, intensive agriculture which is identified by monoculture, and the desire to ensure that farm animals are well fed.

86

Regrettably, this aspect is leading to more greenhouse gas emissions and its even one of the leading generations. To bring this down to your level, the total amount of greenhouse gas emitted from these farm animals and monocultures is equivalent to those issued by all types of transportation available today.

Presently, most folks have realized that the more deforestation done as a result of agriculture claimed more than 20% of the total emissions. Also, land degradation is just another similar sad impact deforestation is causing. And that was just a decade, from the year 2000 - 2010, weighed more than 40 million tons. Why this massive figure?

Simply put, the agricultural sector requires more spaces, that is, lands and there is an everyday increase in the requirement of chemical fertilizers since more demands of agrarian produce have immensely increased. The overreaching impact is causing havoc on forests leading them volatile feeling.

Also, the fluctuation of precipitation will have an impact on water availability or scarcity. It will influence the stress on crops and also have an effect on the availability of water for irrigation purposes. Moreover, when there is no direct and specified forecast of the weather condition, there would be difficulty in planning for farmers.

Furthermore, for more improved yield, the actual absorption of fertilizers and needed minerals by agricultural produce must be at the actual levels. But the changes in temperature and moisture would alter productivity. And definitely, this will have more impact on general productivity. This will be because when plants are unable to get the required threshold for their survival, they tend to be affected in yield. To reveal how severe the situation might turn out to be in the year 2050, there has been a recording of low productivity in the production of rice, potatoes, maize, wheat, and others crops that have been experiencing a decrease.

Undeniably, there are very close relationships between agriculture and climate change. Sadly, it is impacting the way we have much food to feed on, how we have a maximum guarantee on what we are going to feed on. Let's pick the effect on crop and see exhaustively on the impact and how it impacts productivity.

## Effects on Crops

Since crops are dependent on the right amount of temperature and rain, the variation of climate change will harm them. Although, you might not expect to see or experience the disappearance of the crop, probably, steadily. But it could migrate more plants to a higher altitude, more to the mountainside. Water, an essential requirement for crops is rightly needed for proper growth.

For your better understanding, I have compiled five crops, foods that have been impacted by climate rapid change.

*1.Corn*. Being one of the crops that are facing the severe impact of climate change, farmers are having a bad time growing them, and this results in low yield. Farmers need frequent rain to have corns grown in a favorable condition, but what farmers are getting is far from this, rain doesn't come frequently, and even if it eventually rains, it'll have more intense storms, which would not mean good for corns. Sadly, that's not all. The inconsistencies in the rain are leading to excess heat corns suffer from when the heat gets more intense at night.

Buttressing the point further, it is estimated that in Iowa, corn yield is predicted to fall, from 15% to whooping figure of 50%. Stressing it also, there will be a shift in the corn belt region, from the United States to Canada in the coming decades, as expressed by the Vice president for food and market, Jason Clay.

This development will lead to a replacement of corn planting in some region whereby there exists fertile land. The report shows that the part of the Midwest will shift from the farming on corn to growing cotton, Soybeans, etc... What an impact that would be!

*2.Wheat.* Wheat has long served as a means of food for many homes. Additionally, it makes a good source of bread for diabetic and nondiabetic patients. But it's becoming glaring that those who crave for bread from wheat would be forced to turn to another alternative. Why? Hotter temperature from climate change will affect the yield of wheat leading to a shortfall. Countries like India would suffer from the drop in this yield. It has even been estimated that if there occurs an increase in the temperature; in fact, 1 degree will lead to about 8% drop in wheat production.

Unhappily, the uncontrolled climate change will lead to an increase in temperatures, even going beyond the speculated 1 degree. And to halt the havoc would require drastic action, like growing new forest so they can atone for the excess carbon emitted into the atmosphere.

Although the effect of heat loss may not be experienced globally since in warmer region, there might not be any impact on the supply or production. Russia for example, is a more temperate region, they would be capacitated to create more land for the planting of wheat.

*3.Coffee.* Indeed, a freezing temperature wouldn't be suitable for an excellent condition for the growing of coffee, yet, an acute heat wouldn't be an excellent partner too. No wonder growing coffee perfectly will only be done in cool mountainsides, right in the tropic's region.

Take, for instance, the effect of climate change might affect Brazil. The reason isn't unconvincing. The warming of the globe is affecting the region where coffee is grown. Thus, it would not be perfect for the planting of the crops since there will always be heat and consistent rainstorms.

Also, coffee could also migrate to a moderately warm area. But that regions would also not compensate for the loss in production and yield.

*4.Almonds.* If you stay in the U.S., you don't need a soothsayer to tell you that America's source of fresh nuts and vegetables, is California. But lately, something tragic, that even the world will get to know of is coming. America isn't the only beneficiary of almonds; the whole world does; it also serves as the primary source. But California is losing it.

The farms in California are dependent on snow pileup that comes from the winter in the Sierra Nevada mountain; then on melting, it turns to be an essential water source for the country's irrigation canal. But the rapid change in climate has made the situation change, the warming of the environment will make winter comes quickly in the form of rain, and then any fall of snow will melt more rapidly, then farmers are left stranded during the late summer, wreaking havoc on the crops that farmers plant in this region.

Undeniably, from year to year, it has been researched that what is to be expected is that any moist years will be more humid, and more parch years will be dryer. These continuous unfavorable conditions will make shortages of water for farmers to grow crops occur. And for tree crops like almond, it's a bad omen.

**5. *Peaches.*** Peach, which is a fruit tree, has a weird demand for survival. Its experience is that if the peach tree does not have an adequate cold in the winter period, proper blooming is profoundly impacted, drastically. And what does that result into? No bearing of fruits, which does mean that there will be no harvest, at all.

It is accurately estimated that the peach trees that are being presently nurtured in California's Central Valley will demand that there exists a cold hour of nothing less than 750 hours during the winter period.

But, the unfortunate thing about this is that the speculations made by scientists indicate that 10% of the growing area of peaches in California will experience that degree of coldness. Smart breeders might create an alternative, which is, nursing varieties that would require that amount of chilling, yet, there is a little yield of fruit when they get extreme heat during summertime.

Doubting the damage climate change can have on crops, these five crops explained above would convince you. And that's is the reason why I had to go this length explaining five and not just two or three. Well, there is more we can learn about climate change in agriculture. The impact on plants is also not eliminated. Accordingly, lets briefly check the effects of climate change on plants.

## Effects on Plants

Climate change is a danger to the existence of plants since temperature, globally, is always on the increase. The most recent report from the U.S. Environmental Protection Agency shows that carbon dioxide has been the culprit of the most greenhouse gas emissions.

Also, the increase in the amount of warming due to the greenhouse emission has impacted the rainfall events in some regions; there have been more droughts in some areas, this lamentably has led to the extension of some crops being grown. It has led to more changes experienced in the leaf and bloom dates as well.

Rainfall has a towering impact on plants, as their balance suffers in some particular area. When the climate shifts, soil types are negatively influenced. Then it dictates which plant will and will not survive in a region. This makes more species of plants to be left behind, most especially, those types that have long life-cycle. This can change their adaptability rates which in no time, some species might even go extinct, and some would migrate to a more favorable climate weather climate. It can also make more invasive species to adapt rapidly leaving some native species to battle.

So, rainfall, temperature, the duration of the day influences the timing of the plant cycle. Differences in seasons don't leave the plant cycle unimpacted. So, the altered temperature and rainfall due to climate change is causing an extension in growing seasons and leading to the shift as well. Let's check these impacts on pollen allergies, leaf and bloom dates, and additional greenery.

**Pollen Allergies.** Frankly, extended plant seasons would also mean the availability of more pollen. Here is a close example: The ragweed pollen season. Ragweed plants are usually being peaked both in the late summer and early fall, but the plants can keep releasing pollen till the first frost. But now, due to the impact on climate change, dust is now being released right in the early spring and late fall. Ultimately, this leads to longer allergy seasons and pollen counts. By research, they have been experienced in Oklahoma and Southern Canada. In Oklahoma, the Ragweed has an extension of five days, while it is five times more in Southern Canada.

Furthermore, it has been verified that there a change in the cherry blossom trees. It has been experienced that there has been a shift in the peak date. The Cherry Blossom festivals did not even tally or correspond with the peak date in some recent times. The result of climate change is becoming more apparent more than ever before on plants. It impacts where they grow, and failure to thrive due to inconsistencies.

**Changes in leaf.** There are some species of plants that their demand for weather tends to be year after year. A close example is honeysuckles that its first leaf and bloom dates vary from year to year. This type of variation will make it so difficult to identify extreme changes.

From the EPA's climate change, it is revealed that since the beginning of the 2oth century, the growing season has gotten an increase by two weeks in the lower states. In the western region, the rate is about 2.2 days per decade, while in the west of the area, it is approximately one day per decade. Further, nearly all states have experienced a longer growing season.

Besides, the early blooming of plants both in the North and West is also related to the pattern described above. Notwithstanding, blooms happens far on time in some parts of the south. And even in some Southern Hemisphere, the design is more gruesome.

To have a clearer understanding of this pattern, Scientists are assiduously investigating the time when the first buds would surface and when there exists a dropping of leaves. This is the measure to be adopted so that they can correctly get the knowledge about a seasonal pattern. This is being done by making inquiries from cities, towns, and gardens to see how their plants respond to the season.

But, as at present, there is a noticeable change in shift and timing in plants seasons.

**Additional Greenery.** It has been seen that some plants grown in the colder region are becoming more friendly with plants, and the degree is so huge. When a satellite view is used in capturing the area, the greening impact is what is seen all over the northern landscapes. Should that be of concern to anyone? Surely, they should!

This reveals that the vegetation takes in more sunlight as against snow and ice, which means there has been more warming. Besides, there is also a revelation that the melting of tundra discharges methane into the atmosphere. Scientists reveal further that the resultant warmer temperature from climate change will have the ability to destroy tropical forests and when they do, they increasingly emit more gases that are capable of leading to atmospheric warming.

Convincingly, all plant species have their unique responses to climate change. For some species, the sensitivity might be based just on temperature, for some their sensitivity will be based on light, photo-responsive, yet others might still be on natural variability that occurs across all plants. But no doubt, all plants are being affected, they feel the impact of climate change. And as disclosed, if not curbed, more plants will likely go extinct, for some, they would migrate to a conducive climate region with little or zero tolerance in that region.

Crops and Plants are just a part of agriculture which is being impacted by climate change. Livestock which is understood as pet or farm animals that are being reared in an agricultural setting is being negatively influenced by climate change. These domestic animals provide us meat, milk, leather and many more. Learn about how they are being affected, and if you have any, you can learn the best ways to care for them.

## Impacts on Livestock

There is much to learn in this subtopic, impacts of climate change on livestock. You will have a good look at the direct effects, the indirect impact, how it affects livestock production, impact on reproduction, impact on diseases and what to you can do as an intelligent individual.

In the agricultural sector, livestock is one of the significant aspects. It contributes precisely 40% of the farming Gross domestic products. At the global level, the demand for foods derived from an animal is expanding, and it is evident that the livestock sector will have to grow as well. But it is so unfortunate that they are being affected by extreme weather, climate change. The inconsistencies in the changes in climate will reduce the quality and quantity of livestock. Now, it's time you learn about the direct and indirect impact of climate change of animals.

**The Direct Impacts of Climate Change on livestock**

Heat stress is one of the direct impacts of climate change on livestock. This heat leads to a heavy burden on livestock producers, the reason being that they will record reductions in the amount of milk and meat production, health, and the accuracy and effectiveness of reproduction. While a temporary increase in the temperature will directly impact the health of animals. The final result of direct impact is reduced production and economic losses.

**The Indirect Impacts of Climate Change on Livestock**

Well, as there exist direct impacts, there are indirect impacts as well. The records of production droppings are as a result of a decrease in the non-existence of water and feed for maximum growth. Moreover, forage production is also essential for the development of livestock. It has to be both in large quantity and must be of high-grade quality. But as presented by research, forage plants will be impacted on by climate change and global fluctuation of water, and this indirectly will affect how livestock feed on forage.

Also, climate change, has explained earlier has an impact on water demand, both how extended the availability and the quality of water is. And the existence of this irregularity affects water for drinking and agricultural practices. The water deprivation affecting the animal well-being, leading to lower reproductive rates, loss of body weight and more vulnerability to diseases. An example of this is vector-borne disease which could be brought by climate change may severely impact livestock.

## Effect of Climate Change on Livestock Production

As it has been revealed earlier, animals are subjected to heat which will ultimately influence their consumption of feed negatively and reduce the intake of water. The will bring about the malfunctioning of the endocrine system, and which will impact livestock performance. Admittedly, any environmental stressor will influence the weight and daily gain of livestock. For a closer understanding, any reduction in the milk yield in sheep will lead to milk quantity and quality since there will be shortened fat content and some other components making up healthy milk from sheep.

## Impact of Climate Change on The Reproduction of Livestock.

The heat stress from climate change also affects reproduction. As shown, the rate of the conception of a dairy cow may drastically drop by 20-27% in summer, which will lead to a poor impression of oestrus as a result of small estradiol secretion. Also, the heat leads to malfunctioning of the ovarian and embryonic as it will negatively alter the ability of oocyte to be fertilized which will affect the embryo.

Furthermore, the heat stress has been linked closely with the damage of the correct development of the embryo, and the mortality of the majority of embryonic in Cattles. More so, it can lead to slow growth during pregnancy and ultimately, fetal loss. Thus finally, all this combined will lead to reduction in reproduction.

## Impacts on Livestock Adaptation.

Although, some animals try to keep up with the heat stress by adapting their body temperature within their limit, and obviously, this is an essential aspect of survival. But these responses are damaging. The physiological reactions explain an imposed stress on livestock since, without heat, there would not be a need for this mandatory adaptation. And the result? Shortened growth hormone and thyroxin levels.

**The Impact on Livestock Diseases.**

The outbreaks of diseases on livestock are due to the differences felt in temperature and rainfall. Some species functions as vector diseases like ticks and lies that tend to survive throughout the year. Hence, they create the avenue of moving diseases into new areas. And when there exists a new condition, if rain intensifies at that point, it gradually leads to spread. And sure, I need not say that more livestock will be impacted.

But as thing are going, will there be a way to help it? Yes! There are impressive ways.

## What You Should Master

There is no doubt about how climate change impacts on livestock. Since livestock presents and provides man with a decent source of livelihood, then efforts must be taken by everyone to identify them and solve the problem reducing the availability of livestock. There are several strategies to be adopted both now and, in the future, though, but I'll highlight just a few of them.

The government would ensure that relevant technological tool is made available for further investigation and establishment of an early warning system. Then, either as an individual or a group, you should understand the relationships between several stressors for better combat. Also, there must be the establishment of simulation models also, before you keep any animal on your farm, research to check if it's suitable for the environment.

Firmly, if more or new technologies are adopted and introduce into any research that shows the relationship between climate change and livestock, there will exist many ways to curb the menace and get the best from your animal.

The climate change also impacts fisheries as a part of the agricultural sector, before I will speak more exhaustively on the global impact, let's talk about the effects on fishing.

## Impacts on Fisheries

Admittedly, fisheries provide food for a large number of populations living on the planet earth today. And it is daily. Apart from the provision of food, about 10% of the world population are gainfully employed. But sadly, this joy that comes from being comfortably fed on the table -both food and employment is coming to its halt for some individual. How and why?

Marine is under duress! And it is impacting the aquatic life as well. Climate change is the most impactful terror on fisheries. And it is estimated that about $80 billion could be generated from fisheries worldwide if they are well managed or optimized. More to the point, the known "best time" for fishing is becoming history in the warming region, and this will inevitably lead to an economic impact on countries across the world.

Although I've revealed more about the impacts of climate change on water and sea life, this time, I'm going to be more specific about the effects on fisheries. Among conventional agriculture, only fish have the closest link to their ecosystems; It is more apparent and more profound.

There is much evidence that reveals that the impact of anthropogenic climate change is hitting the marine ecosystems. Well, you have to be reminded that usually, climate changes, but in the rapid rate, they lead to both direct and indirect impacts on both marines live physical and chemical factors.

The direct impacts which are reproduction, the adaptation techniques, and physiology and the indirect impact happen around their ecosystem which includes the availability of food, the presence of a predator, competitors, and others.

Marine life is getting it more complicated and trying to survive. And that is owing to the rising temperature which then makes the acidity level of the ocean have an increase. Examples of organisms that combat with this increase in acidity are oysters, shrimps, and the coral (*refer to chapter two*), the acidity level makes it hard for calcification, a process that makes these organisms form their shells. Some animals are at the base of the marine food chain, but sadly they have calcium shells. No life in the sea is left unhindered.

Since the alteration of climate change in the marine food chain is being impacted, there will be severe impact too on the productivity, the composition of species, and distribution. This will also lead to a crash on the ocean. It will affect the grass beds and estuaries that give a home, habitats to the fish.

Take, for instance, a species of fish called Pelagic fish stocks to possess a distinctive space and short-time distribution pattern that is closely associated with the bioclimatic niche. This has led to further revelation knowledge! And the knowledge is that both the shift in primary and secondary production affect the distribution of marine life, their migration habits, and their size.

It should also be noted that some marine species will move right from deep coastal waters and encircling area. And this area is where you have a rapid increase in temperature, leading down into deeper cooler waters. Well, just like some animals, fish also prefer to live around where their forbearance limits are subjected to a range of consideration. Indeed, the increase in temperature, the increased level of acidity, the reduced availability of oxygen and alteration in the salinity will undeniably have a disastrous impact on the population available.

A typical example is seen in the Baltic Sea; there in that region, fish stocks are peculiar in their sensitivity. When hits by climate change, their unique sensibility is leading to their reduction in size. This is owing to salinity and temperature alteration. The last four decades have presented records of visible temperature rise by about 1 degree at the bottom, this has to lead to the withdrawal, and there is almost vanishing of the sub-zero water masses. This action also has made boreal species to migrate northward, and in this area, Arctic fish species occupy the space.

Due to more intensified research, there is a finding of the same attitude in beaked redfish and haddock. Change in climate has led to their north-eastward and poleward migration. But is the region going to make a pleasant home for the existence? No! This movement might lead to the stark extinction of some arctic fish species like the Polar cod. Furthermore, apart from the alteration in their distribution, invasion, and ultimately, destruction of some species, there is a continuous reduction in both size of the fish, and thus the production, since production among new ones will be affected. This critical condition will have an impact on their abundance; then it will impact the ecosystem they explicitly depend on.

Moreover, current flow in the sea and an increase in the temperature will result in shit in the abundance of ocean fish stock too. It will lead to an imbalance, some will enjoy, while some will suffer significantly from the alteration.

In the face of this terror, the individual can play a part. Because climate change isn't the only factor affecting the distributions of fisheries, human activities are playing a role too. Therefore, if you are a fisheries manager, encourage, and you do well to embrace the awareness created by the governments. They are improving new terminologies and regulations as regards how to ensure that fisheries are sustained. There are handbooks designed by the government that will assist fisheries managers in making policymakers all over the world to make the best decision.

Finally, it should be noted, that the existence of aquatic life demand global cooperation; more than ever before, this cooperation is needed. Everyone must respond even apart from the interaction requested by the scientific community. Everyone is involved! Are you willing to be cooperative? That is precisely the motive behind your reading.

Interestingly, there are some technological solutions to helping in the perfect adaptation of agriculture to climate change. Some of the ones that bring powerful solutions are discussed below.

## Technological Options to Adapt

Honestly, when there is a possession of the specific technologies and systems, there will be the restoration of some lost glories due to climate change impact, plus the fact that it will require time and effort.

Science, as a body, has given possible solutions to situation limiting the bountiful harvest of crops and the overall well-being of plants. It should be noted that some regions, a few droughts, as a result of climate change will have a positive impact, yet, if nothing is done to address the areas where the impact is negative, the whole world will experience severe crises. Below are some of the solutions presented through technological options that will lead to better adaptation.

*1. Planting Different Variety of Crop and Species.* Gladly, for most crops today, there is the existence of range. From maturities down to their tolerance. This claim is validated by research conducted. It is evident that wide genetic variability exists between varieties of rice. There are varying responses of these varieties of spikelet sterility in rice.

Also, longer-season cultivars have revealed their adaptability by being steadier while placed under varying conditions. Conclusively, these adapting would thus lead to higher yields or even if losses will be recorded, it will be just a few and little. And this form of responses has been tagged adaptive responses. If farmers, can invest in planting varieties, there will be a drastic reduction in the record of losses.

*2.Seasonal Changes and Sowing Dates.* Frankly, warming of the climate due to climate change is capable of prolonging seasons. Farmers, in turn, should shift into planting crops that have varieties in their maturity so that they can achieve higher yield. Crops with short seasons like oats, wheat, vegetables, and others, when their growing season is being extended, it would lead to more return per annum. Although in subtropical and tropical regions where climate change is impacting their growing season as a result of changes in precipitation pattern, extending the growing season will not do much but will help in preserving the crops and improve yield moderately.

*3.A More Improved Irrigation System.* It has been investigated that areas with more water supply, that is, sprayed agricultural produce have less impact from climate change when compare to dry-land agriculture. However, improving irrigation requires more fund and then it is even dependent on how large water is available. But there is a way out. A method called drip irrigation systems and several other water-conserving strategies would enhance the effectiveness and the functionality of the irrigation system.

And more, to be successful, the management techniques have to be improved, and the price tag on water. When traced down, insufficient supply of water is responsible for the current land degradation facing agriculture today. The more the growing need for water mandates the improvement in management and pricing. Conclusively, tillage method and the addition of crop residues would be an excellent way to generate a more useful supply of water.

*4.Entirely New Crop Varieties.* Crops have varieties when it comes to their genetic base. For some, they have a broader base, yet some have a shallow bottom. The mapping of the new crop will proffer a high potential for survival. It has been studied that new crop varieties would do well under drought and heat. However, this new crop should have been introduced, but profitability, policies by government, and concern for consumers have slowed down the inclusion into the agricultural sector.

*5.Tillage.* Undoubtedly, if tillage is highly reduced, there will be an increase in the crop yield. The consistent growth of cover crops in conjunction with limited tillage and manure crops will present a more possibility of reduction of the effect of soil organic matter. Interestingly, in some parts of the world, they have already embraced these techniques, yet in some regions, they're not even awake to the advantages that surround this option. Therefore, more areas would with no delay embrace this style and techniques as it will do well globally in helping the agricultural sector

**6.More Short- Range Climate Predication Should be Improved.** If there is more reliability in predictions, farmers and growers will be able to make informed decisions, which will affect the dealing and attitude towards crop yields. There should be efforts to make shorter, yet more reliable and dependent predictions. When done, it will allow for reasonable management and more ways to adapt to climate change. The relationship between better agricultural management and projections are closely tied. They make an essential part in all the countries that are improvising it reasonably.

**7.Adjustments in Management.** In taking full control of the excess co2, there must be additional nitrogen and other beneficial fertilizers. When there is much application of nitrogen, there is the tendency that all nitrogen will not be utilized. As a result, they will be leached into the groundwater, thus causing runoff into the surface water. And you will remember, as discussed in chapter two of this book when there is a reasonable amount of nitrogen in the groundwater and surface water, there is a favorable impact on human life, and the marine organisms. So, if these can be adopted, the plant alone will not only be benefiting. Instead, other agricultural produce would.

Conclusively, if at all region, everyone adopts these new technologies and anyone rolled out shortly, there will be expansive change and positive influence on agriculture. This will lead to more yield and balance in the ecosystem will be attained. But apart from these points explained, there is an excellent approach to sustaining agriculture.

It has experimented that agroecology can bring about a drastic change to the impact of climate change. What exactly is agroecology? What solutions exactly does it proffer? Can the world massively turn to it for a lasting solution.? All these and many more are answered below.

## What Help Can Agroecology Proffer?

Should I begin by explaining what exactly Agroecology is? I'm doing that right away! But to understand that, you have to realize what ecology means, should you don't know, let me begin from there, if you know, you can still learn further.

102

Ecology is described and defined as the learning of the relationship between people, animals, plants, their environment and the balance between this relationship. Cleared? Let's move on.

Agroecology is defined as the adoption and application of ecological concepts and principles into agriculture to promote some of the core practices of agriculture. With agroecology, there can be assurance that agricultural practices are sustainable, and the inclusion of local renewable resources are correctly done. Additionally, agroecology adopts the correct use of biodiversity and proffer solution that grants social, environmental and economic benefit. Finally, agroecology provides the adoption of local farmer's preference and intelligence.

But, did you grasp it? I mean what agroecology is all about. In case you don't I'll pick an example, and then I can bring it close to your doorstep.

There are several aspects of agroecology, but for the sake of clarification, I'll explain one, agroforestry. Yes, agroforestry is an example, a perfect example of agroecology.

Agroforestry is identified as the farming system that combines trees and farming. That means you graze your animals, livestock under trees. To what advantage? The trees provide a shelter from the scorching heat and excess carbon dioxide, and gives the fodder too; meanwhile, the livestock enriches the soil. Additionally, when you grow crops under, trees give them the shelter of microclimate for the plants, and the tree returns nutrients to the surface through the tree deep root.

Convincingly, adopting agroforestry is a loved strategy by farmers. It provides them with additional tree crop either timber, biomass or fruit. I'm sure you'd have gotten a clearer understanding of the concept of agroecology.

Furthermore, agroecology is believed to be the way out to improve agricultural systems by either imitating or scaling up natural processes. And this is done to achieve the perfect biological interactions and efficiency of the components of agrobiodiversity. As described above, using agroforestry, agroecology adopts recycling of nutrients on farms, improving communications and productivity via the agricultural system, instead of laying focus on a single species.

Several techniques have been used in agroecology; they have been tested and trusted. This includes integrated nutrients management, agroforestry *(discussed earlier)*, water harvesting, and integration of livestock into farming systems. Taking them one after the other, the first one, integrated nutrients management helps in fixing nitrogen into the soil by fetching nitrogen from organic and inorganic sources of nutrients and limiting losses by erosion control.

The second, agroforestry as discussed is aimed at including many several functional trees into agricultural systems. Water harvesting which is the third one ensures that water productivity of crops is maintained, then, abandoned lands can thus be further cultivated expertly. The final part, integration of livestock into the farming system include the inclusion of dairy cattle, poultry and providing a source of protein to the community and thus keeping the ground fertilized.

All these strategies and techniques include the preservation of agricultural biodiversity since there are many integrations of beneficial factors. Overall, agroecology ensures that the ecosystem is preserved, and climate change is mitigated in the right and perfect way. Check below these four proven and simplified benefits of agroecology and see how deeply they will help in solving the menace from climate change.

*1. It solves The Problem of Yield.* Significantly, agroecology has a high potential for improving yields. In the study conducted, there were comparisons of the impacts of agroecology on 286 agricultural projects in more than 50 growing countries capturing a region of 37 million ha. The result shows that inclusion leads to an increase in yield on more than 12 million farms, at 79%.

*2. The increase of small-scale farmers income.* Since agroecology relies basically on locally produced inputs, all the nutrient-starved soil, degraded soil and soil that requires replenishment will be served to the brim. Farmers would not have to purchase different fertilizers at an exorbitant price; instead, they will add livestock manure within reach. They can adopt the planting of trees that do an excellent job in taking nitrogen out of the air, attaching it to the leaves and will be transferred into the soil. All of these will reduce farmers' lending of money to purchase some external inputs since most of what is needed in getting their yield is within their reach. Hence, the income will be magnified!

*3.Contribution to the Development of Rural Areas and Several Economy Sectors.* Indeed, agroecology contributes to the advancement of rural development; it is identified as relatively- labor-intensive. It is best practiced on a small plot of land, for maximum yield. Why the first part is labor intensive is because of the complication of the task from managing several animals and plants. Nevertheless, as times progresses, it reduces. The nature of the work presents employment opportunities in rural areas, it limits and discourages much of the rural-urban migration

*4. Nutrition Increase is Certified.* Sadly, the mandatory boosting of crops is one-sided; the foods are mostly carbohydrates - maize, wheat, and rice. Even, the availability of over 75,000 plant species presents human with protein and an abundant amount of energy. Today, there is more shift as nutritionist insists on varieties of nutrients-based result from farming system. Gladly, agroecology system can proffer this solution accurately.

Finally, agroecology is capable of providing different help to the ecosystem. It helps in creating a balanced habitat for wild plants; it does beyond that and helps pollination, it assists in water supply and, additionally, it brings more resilience to the agricultural biodiversity, also it helps is reasonable mitigating climate change. Presently, there is no doubt that agroecology would ensure a lasting solution in the ruin done by climate change, and when it is being scaled up, more will be done. So, when asked if agroecology will pave the way for curbing the negative impact of climate change, I'm sure your answer will be as right as yes!

Is there a way to link climate change impact on the economy? I'm confident that if you've been reading from the beginning, you would have noticed that different impression discussed have a close-link to the economy either of the country impacted or globally. Notwithstanding, experts have spoken so extensively on climate change impact on the economy; shorelines, industries, technology, migration, and sadly, the collapse of the economy! Shocking? That's why the effect has to be learned. Thus, we can see how we can contribute our quota.

## Chapter Five

# Climate Change and The Economy

### How it Operates

By now, would you deny the impact of climate change on the environment? It's very likely you would. Most especially, if you've started your reading from the beginning. But just like many individuals, realizing the grip of climate change is just coming to them, a solidly firm understanding has not been gotten. And before I delve fully into the growth zones -as related to climate change and economics, the effects on shorelines, industry, technology, migration, the global economy and the possibility of climate change wrecking the economy system, it is mandatory that I describe and explain vividly how climate change and economy works or operates.

The reality is that there are several facets of the economy that are under the threat of climate change. The energy resources, infrastructures - both governments and private, and labor productivity are an example of where climate change is impacting.

Adopting several modeling, advanced researchers are finding out how global warming, a result of climate change is impacting the economy. These are ways in which climate change could intensify the impact on the economy.

> 1. The already fertile land hits by climate change will result in a drop-in yield, limiting sales and abundance of food in the economy.
>
> 2. A road plied by several road users, but as a result of climate change - hurricane, rising of sea level lead to flooding which has to be returned into its actual state, more fund will go into the reconstruction.
>
> 3. The power sectors -will be discussed thoroughly in chapter six, would require spending more millions of dollars to build a

more reliable and functional to oppose severe weather - from climate change.

Summarily, agriculture, transportation, and energy are the leading aspects gulping millions of dollars in the economy.

Explaining each further, the decrease in the farmland will result in long-term loss of the economy's high-yield capacity. And honestly speaking, this is more devastating than other forms of the economic downturn, because there is still going to be an expectation that when things get better, the company or industries will bounce back to work.

For the reconstruction of road facilities, it can be expensive. It will require carving a critical fund that might have been utilized into something much more reasonable; they can be used in handling other essential aspects of the economy. It is a drawdown!

The last one though could bring about new yield, but as the climate change grows intense, it is very likely that more money will be disbursed into the power sector to meet up with the growing demand. And what is the assurance that such an upgrade would stop? And will it come at no extra cost and zero impact on economic stability?

Top of that, everyone's income will suffer shipwreck since climate change will impact or claim 10% of the Gross Domestic Product (G.D.P). Although, the impact rate or level may vary since the impact of climate change is not uniform all over the world. So, the type of work, where some residents' lives will play significant roles.

As an example, a flood-prone region will be at very high risk, it could become uninhabitable, or if lived, the condition will not be favorable. More so, many companies will have a massive strike, if workers or the facilities erected will be impacted by flooding as a result of climate change. Even though, when it comes to adapting, some would find it easier than some, everyone will be affected. Since some individuals will be able to migrate easily to areas that are less stricken by climate change, others with no means will not be able to.

There is so much risk facing a large number of people. Granted, we are excellent when it comes to adaptability. Yes, we can do it! Travel back to centuries when people had no luxuries offered by advancement in technology. But what do we see now? The advent of these things. The development that comes around changes how we live and what we use in simplifying our living. All these can mitigate how we react to climate change, defining how the impact is lower and lesser on the economy.

But even human's adaptation might suffer other hiccups. Since the alteration happens at an exceedingly speedy rate, an adjustment that on a regular scale would have taken a considerable length of time would not match up with the time when changes are experienced or seen, this, in turn, can lead to the death of some since they will have a problem adapting before another change set in.

What do you think will happen when climate change hits the common staple food crops and thus they are being wiped off by severe weather? Will that not be a massive strike hitting individual and the economy at large?

Even in the 21st-century economy, climate change is impacting it significantly. Yes, it is never an understatement or gainsaying to assert that climate change is having an impact on the economy.

In the next sub-topic, we will explain how the growth zones are being exceedingly influenced. Do you even have an idea about the growth zone? Why not let us journey down together?

### What is the "Growth Zones"

Fittingly, this sub-heading comes as a question. I see a chill of relieve, isn't it?

Growth zones are defined as a region where some category of plants are animals are capable of growing and living comfortably, or their tendency to withstand the temperature of the zone.

When climate changes severely, leading to warming of the planet, the temperature, that is, the average temperature of different regions

109

experience a rise. The extended impact is terrific, and why? Check this illustration:

Imagine you've been sitting under a shelter made of zinc with no overlay at the base, evidently, in the early hours of the day, you will find it extremely a cool place to relax, but as the sun starts to rise, temperature definitely will change, grow, and when its finally noontime, will you still find it conducive to stay? Definitely no! And at that time, you will only be left with two options: either you stay and bear the heat or seek another cooler and comfortable shelter. Any wise, intelligent individual will choose the later!

This briefly highlighted illustration explains what organism would do when faced with the unbearable condition. Microhabitats, which serves as a home for varying species of plants to thrive excellently will move when a non-conducive environment encounters them. Research has even explicitly told how they migrate; they have been recorded to walk near the poles of the earth. In extreme cases, they have been left vulnerable; as a result, vanishes and extinction of species is the inevitable end.

An example is the Fauna that has continually evolved over the years to thrive in the microhabitat, but when they are also faced with severe temperature increase, they have been seen to either migrate with the microhabitat and adapt or die out. And continually, more plants will be heading for extinction, leaving the growing of new species in the new habitat zones. If you still haven't known how it affects the economy, below is a more comprehensive explanation.

The shift and extinction of some plants will negatively impact farming. It may turn out to be that areas, where crops have been entirely grown, will turn too

dry or become wetter for plants in that region. The city used for cultivation of vegetables would be impacted; it will change. Areas nearer to the poles that have been either too cold now would be suitable for cultivation of plants, while the region, previously known to bearable will be boiling, and at that, they will not be favorable for planting. In all land,

land available for cultivation will be scarce, impacting the production of crops.

For some animals, with a closely-linked symbiotic relationship with humans will continue and maintaining their present location. Notwithstanding will have no option than either to proceed with migration or have to die while searching for survival under a favorable condition, atmosphere! It might lead to the entire disappearance of some habitat for wild animal survival. You will still recall some of the animals that I highlighted in the previous chapter, chapter two precisely, the disappearance of these animals will lead to more hit on the economy.

## Shorelines

From the previous chapter, you already know that climate change is making the ocean level rise. And when ocean level rises, there is no doubt the shoreline will have a twist or a difference as well. Although due to natural, positive change in the time past, say, centuries ago, the coastlines have changed their course, nevertheless, human intervention, the contribution to the speeding up of the rapid climate change and it's knocking us down. Take a complete look into what has happened in the Sahara and Mesopotamia region. These regions, thousands of years ago, were lusher (greener), but regrettably, it has turned dried! They are becoming a desert plain.

Due to the massive impact, this increase in the sea level is to bring both now, and in the future on the economy, coastal managers, occupants in the coastal regions and government itself are concerned mainly about this problem. So many questions that answers were needed to is to know precisely what will be the scale of the impact? How it is likely to translate into local problems, the precise measures that can be adopted, and when is it right to withdraw from the shoreline, rather than defending one's property and lastly, how relevant and real are the information gotten regarding the impact of sea level on human existence.

Adaptability of humans will create a new development of infrastructure. How do I mean? The ocean level rise will make inhabited area along the shores of the ocean to become underwater, and for those

111

whose wealth would not want them to migrate from there, they may turn to engineer, architect to design a structure that can withstand that present condition. Even though only a few will try this, the majority of folks will migrate. Did you see the hit on the economy?

Well, the matter of constructing new homes, destroying regular ones. Additionally, cities that have found themselves on the shore will heavily sink money into erecting dikes and other several water management systems. And if you are recent about the development that goes on with the climate change impacting the economy, you'd remember, in a bit to ensure the safety of its residents, Netherlands and Venice erected dikes and restructure and scaled up water management policies. Imagine how much money will be invested into this?!

Up till now, places, companies that have been battling with this water crises have already been equipped with technological tools to wrestle this, but you may wonder why are they fighting instead of completely migrating like some of the counterparts, within their possessions they have money to push in, for long term, they worth investing to.

But, at the peak of an unfortunate situation, where it is not confident that what is invested in solving the issue will eventually yield a positive result in the long run, or if it's signaling that a dead end, these set of folks will migrate. Will this mean well for the host community? Even though there might seem to be more extension, there will be a record of competition for the land area where edifices would be built, and that's even if that will not open up a new way for havoc from climate change.

There are more ways to respond to sea level rise. Over the years though, how science understands the susceptibility, and adaptability techniques regarding sea level rise has tremendously increased. Soon, it is so bad that some regions have been projected to have a more significant impact, like developing areas, the reason is owed to a vulnerable population and weak or zero adaptive techniques. Which institution is responsible for the scaling up and protection? The economic institutions take the lead, and it is wise they adopt technological tools, carve out knowledge resources and other relevant organization in ensuring the life of the masses is sustained and preserved.

Nevertheless, developed countries are not even immune to the impact of sea level rise. Even in the U.S., there are still more to be learned as regards the effect and more adaptive measures to be utilized. Also, some models have great potentials, transferring them to actual, real adaptive techniques is still a problem to be wrestled with. Additionally, some technological remedies are not even plausible in some locations and adopting them in that location will further impact the coastal ecology, aesthetics, tourism, and other essential factors.

Even though at present, many are erecting new structures, raising their existing building above the level of flooding, and many other suggested measures exist, there are rarely used since there are underground incentives and many other reasons like necessary protection and many cases of emergency.

Similarly, some hindrances are making the exact solution to be very challenging; some of these are the withdrawal from the shoreline, land use and others. These sets of limitation on how humans can adapt well are affecting existence. It must be seen that numerous investigations are out now, in seeking a way out in combating the damage faster sea level rise is bringing. More inquiry to be made should significantly be to ensure that the solutions are socially welcomed, it's cheap, and the most efficient way. If it is not cost effective the results will be felt by the economy of the country, or region adopting that style. And if the result isn't socially accepted the money pumped into the research will amount to nothing; it will be a waste.

Therefore, before research is done, there must be a gathering of high-rank officials, intellect, and renowned individuals with reinforced understanding about climate change impact on shorelines, and the economy. This is to ensure positiveness is firmly established.

**Industry**

When an industry is established in a country or region, it boosts the growth of the community and those near rapidly, but when there is a concentration of industries, that is, many industries in a region, automatically it spans to make so much more impact. As defined by economy gurus, industrialization is picked as one of the essential economic development that has happened to humans in history. Amazing, not so? There is no doubt!

Sadly, all these glories are sinking and dying. Yes, that is the correct, climate change is impacting industrialization, and that is hitting a sharp blow on the world's economy. Climate change will affect industrial raw materials supplies and all the procedures utilized. You might need to be entirely convinced. Yes, I've got you served too. Let's proceed!

What has happened and is happening in Finland's industrial sector will be used in driving home the point deeper. Why Finland exactly? The raw materials in Finland solely rely on weather and several changes in the natural habitat. For a very long time, industrial production has played a significant and core role in boosting the economic growth of the country, Finland. Take, for example, for more than seven (7) decades, that is, from 1925 to 2000, there was a record of immense growth, that it is being recorded that percentage increase is near 6% on a low yearly. Isn't that remarkable? And what could be accountable for this reduction? We shall see soon.

But, now, in the 21st century, the story, record, statistics have changed, drastically! The speed of growth that is being sung has receded, slowed down, in fact, at a degree that was never imagined. To tell the extent of severity in stagnancy, the percentage growth has been below three percent.

In total, it is approximated that more than 400,000 people are employed in the industrial sector in Finland. As each day passes by, there has been a shift in the concentration of the industry, they have shifted from the paper and wood company to the processing of equipment machinery. And if deep checked today, one of the most vital sectors of

114

the industry is the electronic and electrical equipment. Consequently, this improvement is coming down to industries that their raw materials are minimally impacted by climate change, that is an excellent move though. But it doesn't end there!

Since the global economy is closely linked with the economy, climate change will impact on both the forest industry and the free food industry, these two, are essential for the adequacy of food in the country.

Furthermore, natural resources, that is, the forest is subject to excellent weather condition. And in Finland, this aspect is one of the most impacted sectors today. There has been recent development of increased precipitation migration of animals, plants toward the north pole, and other factors - related to climate change are impacting the life of forests in several ways. It is investigated and discovered that if these are left to take their course, these changes wouldn't be as rapid as this, and at that slow rate, there would have been a better way to adapt without causing more harm. Specifically, in its natural shift or change, climate zone is expected to shit from 150-550 kilometers north just in this present century alone, more so, trees' natural movement is just a simple distance of 20-200 kilometers just in a century too.

The extreme drought would likely lead to wildfire, and more wind damage is projected at a very high degree. Climate change is also capable of impacting not only the raw materials but industrial processes too. Examine how:

When there is a reduction in the ground frost, it hinders logging during the winter period. This, in turn, exposes the trees reserved in the forest during the falling to be damaged. There is more, road condition resulting from melting snow will emerge into difficulty, the ground frost will mandate that timber and machinery used are well kept.

The durability of wood felled from the forest will be impacted. They will be influenced by extended growing duration and excess carbon dioxide in the air. Thus, the workability will be affected; it might create the use of new tools and other essential material that will be able to work on them as against some of the current one used. Frankly, the impact of climate change will also affect the types of raw materials that are provided for the food industry.

Further, the impact of climate change will also extend to the construction industry. Climate change has brought about fresh challenges that are reaching the construction industry. It is being experimented that changing weather, especially the severe ones, is requesting for the addition or improvising new types of construction materials. These are owed to damp condition that repeatedly changes, the frequency of storms and the defrosting of the ground.

More to the point on the impact of climate change on construction is that the rainy weather will assuredly lead to high risk of damage to the structures and more increase in the drying of some compositions. In severe weather, the health of an individual working under that condition will be at risk. Top of it, the severity of climate change is set to reduce the pacing at which engineers work in the site.

In the industrial sector, is the energy supply and safety facilities are embedded *(see chapter six)*. The industry is also if not fully affected are partially affected by the factors that are impacting residential buildings. Take for example the use of air-conditioning and heating facilities industries. There might be more demand for the air conditioning, while there would be reduced demand in the heating facilities since there is sever heat. Will this not bring the need for heating facilities, thus a decreased in the sales.

Over and above that, another part that will also hit the industry, reaching the sector is the alteration in the obtainability and national emergency disbursement. When there is a rise in the problem emerging from bodies of water that is becoming warmer this is likely to influence, retard the application of water for cooling industries. It shouldn't come as amazement if industrial plants that are specialized in transporting inflammable gases are razed with fire since they are at high risk of light due to extreme weather condition. In sharp contrast, there can see the advent of excessive rainfall may retard and influence the operation of the industrial plant; they may be corroded and rust off.

The logistics industry will also be placed under severe attack. First when the severity of rain happened many areas will be flooded, and this might lead to a slow pace of delivery of materials and total halt of the process until government officials solve the situation. In some cases, transporting of some good might be damaged since they will be prone to accident and several other hindrances.

Well, as at present, research is being made into understanding all the direct impacts of climate change on the industry and other indirect effects. Well, it has only been established that there is no significant immediate impact of climate change on the industry. There are still little done to remedy the indirect effects on the industrial sector. Well, as the world progresses in understanding and research, there is more to be done. There are more data to be getting that will execute more eloquent result in pointing to a roadway to solving the impact of climate change on construction, energy, chemical, metal raw materials and the processes involved in making it work.

It should be noted that over the year, before the severe impact of climate change, human have been utilizing fewer resources to achieve more. So, more work needed to be done so that the use of fossil fuels will be reduced, and more pressure should be mounted on industries so for them to become more efficient. One way is holding industries responsible for any energy reckless extravagance. Also, more individual should be keen on using resources more efficiently. Effectiveness will be maintained since power itself is one of the leading sectors of the economy. And if many people are waking up to the impact of climate change, it will become more vital. Well, to a reasonable degree we can fight the war if we have consensus agreement and follow every right step carved by both individual government and the world at large.

I'm assured that you have seen the impact of climate change on industry and how it is connected to the economy. There is another aspect worth learning; this aspect is the technological aspect of the world. Well, in this section you shall see whether there will be some pros, advantages climate change can make technology bring down to our doorsteps or its impacting technology negatively.

## Technology

Commendably, there will be a more positive side of technology than the negative side as climate change will have an impact on technology. Because as at present, the demand for new technology is growing at an unprecedented rate. This is done so that there will be a more excellent way of arresting carbon dioxide and methane. For example, in the region of Siberia, excess methane will be emitted into the atmosphere, and according to scientists, if there is more methane, it can do capture the warmth, even more than how carbon dioxide will do. So, excess methane in the atmosphere will result in warmer with more impact on the economy, positively! Could this be true?

I think that as this condition grows intense, more technologies will be developed to cater for the catering for the excess methane. Indeed, going this way will be valuably undertaken.

More technological innovations that might have a tremendous impact on the growth of the economy is the creation of renewable energy like wind, a geothermal source, and others. Therefore, more power would be developed to solve the issue of global warming from climate change.

There is no gainsaying whatsoever that new technology will emerge, and when they do, more money will be generated in the technological sector - at least good news, isn't it? Moreover, the money to be made due to the impact of climate change on human and using technology to remedy some will be huge. To prove that my assertion is not baseless or mere on wishful thinking, below are some of the technological tools that will be designed in the future to combat the issue of climate change. As you read see the potential these tools have in contributing to the economy, and how they are changing human vulnerability to climate change impact.

*1. Big Data.* This is an incredible way of creating or generating awareness. The awareness is to inform the majority of people about the unfavorable impact of climate change. And interestingly, the UN recently declared a global competition called the Big Data Climate Challenge. This incentive is to ensure the use of large data is combating the issue. Their recently released projects reveal the economic consequences of climate change.

*2. Mobile Apps.* To design an application that will take the full course of making daily changes possible is indeed demanding a real work. But happily, they are out in the world being utilized by people that have seen how they can minimize their risk and help the world at large.

*Oroeco* is an app that is designed to monitor your carbon footprint efficiently. It accomplishes that by insisting on carbon on every purchase, what you consume, do and comparing you with people within your community. PaperKarma is also an application that its specialty is found on how best to utilize paper. It expertly cut your paper waste.

*GiveO2,* the last to be mentioned is applied to monitor your carbon footprint as you move from one region to another. How to use the app requires that as soon as you begin your journey, turn it on, automatically, it will calculate your carbon utilization. If your usage is high, you can gladly offset it.

*3. Clean Energy.* One of the biggest menaces that need to be tackled is clean energy. Storage and transmission of power after it has been acquired still hold to be an immense challenge. And in ensuring that a smarter grid is built, technology has to offer a helping hand. The impact will be to utilize renewable energy means.

*4. Meal Replacement.* Did you know that it requires more energy and power to prepare a burger than to sufficiently power approximately seven iPads? What does this mean? The livestock industry happens to be a significant contributor to climate change. But technology is making it stress less to the avoid animal-based meal. Shortly, there will be a development of a technique known as Beyond Meat, a plant protein that has an identical look and taste like meat.

**5. *Geoengineering.*** Some would gladly refer to it as planet hacking. But why? It's only because it adopts the hacking of the planet, extracting the resources and using it to bring about new solutions. This technological style is established on the notion that climate change can have a halt when they use efficiently, human-made techniques. The major aspects are limiting carbon dioxide, and solar radiation. Some group of experts though call this a controversial pattern since they are unsure as to how most of its basic ideas will have health effects and benefit the earth.

***Open Source management.*** More research will be done in ensuring sustainability. One of the ways to accurately achieve that is through open data and open source technological development. And amazingly, the US government has made access to recent data about climate change available to everyone in search for it. This will let many researchers form a basis to further their research, know the stage of research, and get to see what has been accomplished.

***IoT.*** The real function of IoT is ensuring at individual levels water is saved, and again, it leads you to take an alternate route to avoid excess use of gas, and non-productive driving. In a sense, the function is to ensure a smarter use of energy.

***Mapping.*** The science backing up this move is remarkable. It is impressive and rewarding. U.S Geological Survey recently, barely a month old released a 3D elevation Program that cost approximately $13 million. This is created to facilitate standard and advanced mapping. It will further assist in providing flood maps, and the most reliable areas for farming.

***Data Centers.*** Many companies have been claiming the use of renewable energy. Google uses 34% right now and they claim to have an upgrade soon. For a company like Apple, they claim using 100%

renewable energy. All of these are a good way of restructuring the impact of climate change on the economy.

## Migration

Even though some individuals can adapt to the impact of climate change, it is not everyone that can endure the severe weather event, variable temperature, an increase in the sea level, especially, for those that stay on the sea coast. Inability to experience this situation will lead to harnessing a new surviving plan; a more productive way from suffering. And the report has it that one of the most common solutions to this problem since the Era of severity is Migration! They seek a new home and a new habitat.

And indeed, these sets of people moving from one region where they experience a terrible climatic condition or where they heard the report of a climate change consequences that might necessitate their migration from that region to a more favorable climate region are referred to as climate migrants.

Before I proceed further, at least, more in-depth, let me explain the connection between climate change and migration. Then, the sub-topic itself to will come vivid and explicit!

Regardless of what some might hold as an opinion, believing that people would migrate due to climate change is reasonable and logical. Although, some might imagine, how would climate change lead to me leaving my preferred territory, where I have gained more relevance and invested in. Some would think, why can't they develop a better form of adaptability. Some who doubts the idea might even believe that those who claim to migrate due to climate change might have a more profound reason, hidden from the public.

But let me ask you could these objections be close to the truth? Well, your answer will solely depend on how convincing you find the following points.

Although, in gaining a shred of reliable evidence to support the link between migration and climate change, there are scientific data that could be referred to as been tricky and unclear. But there is a light that's brimming to clarity and relevance. In Europe, there is substantial research that points to a convincing proof that a severe change in climate change will lead to migration; in fact, if not terrific.

Take, for instance, in a study that's been recently released in the science journal, facts gotten from the United States have shown that there have been changes in the applications submitted for asylum. There's been a link to the European Union from the beginning of the year 2000 and 2014. These applications feature weather abnormality. How? There was investigation made to reveal that from over 100 countries where applicants come from; it is evident that there is a definite link between the applicant from a particular state and difference within the temperature of that country.

Precisely, it has been shown that asylum application to the EU had a low rate in the country where they a have a moderate temperature, say, 20°C, and in sharp contrast, had an increase in either extreme coldness or hotness. Isn't this a roadway? Definitely! It goes a long way to reveal that climate change has an impact on the rate of immigration. And that's a green light to authenticating the prove.

That's not all! More proves rolled in too. The researcher further used the data gotten to make a prediction, with what goal? To discover how future climate change would impact the inflow of immigrants in Europe. And to what result? It's astounding!

The data shows that with an increase in global warming, from climate change, given, a moderate level of growth in temperature, the number of asylum applicants to the European Union would have approximately 28% rise. Between 2000 and 2014, the average application yearly was above 300,000, but the 28% increase will lead to an approximate figure of 450,000 applicants. And top of it, where severe weather conditions were considered, they validated that the percentage increase would be around 188%, and that will yield about 1 million applicants yearly.

Now, which angle will you tend? Aren't you entirely convinced of the severe impact climate change will have on migration?

Although, it should be noted that these estimations (that of 28% and 188%) could be excessive, due to the reason that no one can accurately say this is what is going to happen and again, as time passes by humans may develop a more intricate and way of adapting. But don't forget, the bases where these predictions are based are real and what is currently happening.

Nevertheless, the figures and predictions might also be too low, since climate change may develop more intense weather Events, thus making more people migrate than the expected rise in the future.

Currently, the European Union are striving hard to execute a form of adaptation that will fit those new settlers. And if at all, the figure grows more rapidly, they might be issues of pressure mounted on the complex exist immigration service in the continent.

As at today, Europe is still identified as one of the appealing destinations for those migrating due to extreme weather conditions. The reason is far from economic stability and the less impact of climate change. Nevertheless, apart from the European countries, the world at large too will have a feel of migration due to climate change. Maybe folks will move from one state to a less impacted state.

Another research has even suggested that more immigrants will come from Mexico, Caribbean and other regions to Canada and the United States. Similarly, the impact of climate change in the Pacific region that is leading to a rise in sea level will lead to the migration of some individuals to places like New Zealand. And so exciting is that the government of the country has bent on creating a visa, dubbed climate refugee visa to cater for the accommodation of future immigrants.

Finally, viewing from a continent and global scale, there is more evidence that climate change would impact migration. And when residents of a country move from one region of severe weather event, the area where they moved off will have a severe economic impact; there will be a change.

## Global Economy

Verifying the effect of climate change on the global economy strictly is of paramount importance. It will become the mouthpiece to what the world is to face in the future as regards the impact of climate change on various aspects of the economy. This would mean either to improve the awareness of the havoc, or there should not be any reason for panic.

Inflation, energy cost, and insurance are an essential aspect of the economy that verifying how the impact of climate change will be is highly needed. For a fact, the climate change impact on the economy will be extended. However, while there might be positivity, for example in the technological sector, most results will be negativity. And again, it will be widespread, hence the use of the term "global." Also, as long as there are damages due to properties, reduced in productivity, security threats and mass migration, there will seem to be more infliction of negativity than advantages.

According to researchers, climate change is projected to keep increasing every day. Take into concern what happened in New York, during the Hurricane Sandy, what becomes of many properties worth millions of dollars? They have swept away. Remember I mentioned three aspects of the economy that I will be diving into, namely, inflation, insurance, and energy. I'll check each section successively. Let me start with the increase in price of commodity.

### How Climate Change Will Affect Inflation

Climate change will not solely bring about a change or reduction in output. unfortunately, it will have a global impact on the general price level. And that itself, will move man into inflationary effects of climate change.

For instance, the agricultural yield is highly sensitive to any slight change in weather, and when they become more extreme - more drought, excess rainfall, crop yields will have a reduction, and in a sector where

124

production of food is of high importance they suffer, impacting country where they export to. And for scarcity, they will increase in the general price of produce. And what happens to a consumer's income? They spend more to purchase. Although, since not all regions will have the same impact, there might be an increase in some yield regardless of that, the area affected is more than those moderately affected, and with an increase in warming, the price of food commodities will rise.

Another reason why inflation may occur is the aspect of land scarcity as a result of the hit from climate change. This continual increase in some weather events may lead to migration; that is, some areas where lands have been cultivated before will become inhabited. Consequently, political and socioeconomic consequences will yield more increased demand for insufficient land for cultivation. And how will living feels like, difficult! We will be congested. And the prices of the commodity in that region will increase.

**How Climate Change Will Impact Energy Cost**

Since there might be an increased energy bill, these might build the idea of inflation. The increase in the intensity of climate change may make a demand for energy to cool down the heat during summer. There would as well be a need to purchase heating facilities during harsh winters. Well, if I talk on energy demand only, I won't forget to highlight the reduction in the supply. And the primary reason will be that climate change will impact how the power stations, functioning one is being run, as temperature goes higher.

Recently, we've been seeing that governments are making a move to foster the adoption of green energy by the masses. But this move will further lead to inflation. This is because taxes will be paid on all the fossil-fuel gotten from electricity. And bear in mind that energy is used in producing all needed in the world. The increase in the price of energy will be felt globally.

125

**Climate Change is Impacting Insurance.**

Insurance is going higher. And one of the things to blame mostly is climate change. The insurance company itself has revealed how its recent understanding has shown that they would be impacted by climate change. The effects have been felt on profits. The impact of extreme weather in the U.K and U.S has led to damage of properties, and to cover for the cost, the insurance company has spent much. For example, the report shows that in the year 2011, the insurance company paid a considerable sum of $126 billion to cover for the natural disaster that happened. When a top official, Mark Carney, The Governor of the bank of England was speaking on the research made by the Bank relating to the expenses incurred, it was gathered that one of the leading risks the Banking industry faces is climate change.

Thus, the insurance company has sorted out a way to solve the issue. One of the ways they've employed is increasing the cost of insurance. For instance, the cost of flood insurance has doubled from what it used to be in the past. Accordingly, the increase in the cost of insurance will also impact inflation; this will stop companies from establishing in regions where there would be a high risk of impact from climate change.

Judging from this situation, many business decision and plans are not leaving behind climate change - what shows how deadly global economy is being impacted. Sadly, if this goes worse, the insurance company may fail to grant insurance cover, and if this happens, the government will be at a very high or they would be mandated at all cost to seek for a lasting way of mitigating.

Regional effect of climate change impacting the economy is also undeniable. Sadly, the developing countries will be hit the most. Naturally, some regions have a warmer climate in the developing world; they depend solely on sectors that are highly sensitive to the impact of climate change - agriculture, tourism, and forestry. With the increase in temperature -due to climate change, Africa will experience an intense drop in agricultural yield. Thus, there will tend to be insufficient food livestock for consumption. But at the call, or cry for help, they might turn out to developed countries for help, but sadly, the developed countries are being affected too.

If in the developed country they can work out their problem efficiently, they will want to satisfy their citizens, before listening to the call for help. Why most developed land will be able to withstand some of the effects of climate change is because they have capital to pursue solid research and come up with a solution. However, developing countries will have difficulty ensuring quality research, since they don't have fund to make that work.

Besides, the severity of this situation in developing countries will have a bearing on government budgets. Those who feel the impact of the natural disaster -from climate change are often the people in a position of authority. They are responsible for the assurance of well-being of their citizen. They are mandated to clear away the remnants of natural disasters; what would cost lots of money. They are also mandated to provide relief support and health care facility that will be of help to the member of the community. It might also be recorded that there would be revenue reduction - this will from countries that are solely dependent on tourism for migration.

From the above point, you should be able to understand these vital points: One, when developed countries feel the consequences of climate change, the resources giving to developing countries to serve as aid will be reduced since they - the acquired land will be mostly concerned about increasing the struggle on domestic budgets.

Two, governments of the developing nations will have no options than to spend more of the resources, channeling at battling and wrestling the cost of severe weather change, a fund that would have been used in pursuing more productive projects. Ask me, how would they not be affected?

Additionally, note that such an impact will even extend to a long- term project. Moreover, these countries, developing countries would have only little resources to build a stronger economy. And another aspect to consider in the issue of climate change impacting the economy is that, when a tragedy- caused by climate change, occurs, the time that will be spent in the restoring of what was lost, recover, and getting back to a stable economy will be longer than when the issue occurs.

Correctly, if a disaster strikes in a day, evacuating those affected will apparently not last a few days, government intervention in building a relief shelter will possibly not take a few days, restoring the area of disaster, that is, if there would not be another future occurrence will take more time, needless to talk about how the government will regain the money spent on the event.

But, among all the developing countries that are more liable to attack, the region of Asia and Africa are more impacted. Sub-Saharan Africa and South East Asia are going to be the most hit as indicated by the World Bank. And, the intense flooding, cyclones that have been beating Mumbai, in south Asia, points the assertion to be true.

Also, the disappearance of snowmelt will lead to a reduction in the flow of water. In Vietnam too, a center for tourism all over the world will have some of its region susceptible to climate change. For example, the part where rice is mostly produced, Mekong Delta is set to experience a rise in sea level, and if this happens, more of the areas used for growing rice will suffer disaster.

The situation in the Sub-Saharan region would be food security which will pose more challenge as a result of drought and a substantial shift in rainfall pattern. Another, worthy of note point is that many developing countries are located in low latitude, and according to recent estimations, more than 75% of the damages brought by climate change are from these regions. Contrasting this unfavorable impact in these regions, areas like Canada and Europe would have a high yield in agricultural produce and several benefits which will boost the economy of the country.

In the wake of these challenges, there should be better responses to the call of climate change. Organizations, governments, shareholders and every individual at the grass root should bring heads together and discuss how they can effectively mitigate the effect of climate change. Going by the output from research, carbon dioxide emissions is one of the leading reasons for a change in climate. As a result, there should be a decision to make up policies that will reduce how this gas is being emitted. If there is no establishment of public policy, the economy, the global economy will be moving toward the verge of collapse. Also, to ensure strictness, the government would motivate and penalize. Confused?

It is often said if you would want people to do what is right, you would either motivate them, either by subsidizing the rate at which they make purchase of green resources, or get money in return to abiding by the rules laid down in order to oblige or give penalty, that is punish any firm or individual that fails to meet up with the demand. This might include locking up and placing an embargo on anyone found guilty.

As explained earlier, climate change is liable to reduce economic growth and ultimately lead to inflation. This will place the world bank in a severe dilemma.

Finally, seeing the impact climate change could have on the global economy would result in a better way of solving the problem. Remember that if a weather event grows extreme shortly, the economy will be weakened. There will be damage to capital stock, productivity, labor supply, and others.

Since the essential parts of the economy has being discussed, I'll be expanding your understanding on what most of the world's production is dependent on - energy!

Energy and climate change relationship is indeed a broad topic, hence, the next chapter has been dedicated exhaustively to discuss more on energy - the demand and supply, water availability and relationship with power, wind speed and renewable, how electricity is being placed at high risk and getting a valid result on whether there is a need to boost renewable or it is growing at an unprecedented rate and lastly, other impressive ways to scale up the electricity sector.

**Chapter Six**

# Climate Change Impacts on Energy

## Overview

Have you ever felt bad because you couldn't get the right energy needed in accomplishing a task? If you have, you aren't alone. Everybody depends on power for one function or the other. No wonder, power is regarded as an essential aspect of our life! It plays a vital role. It is with energy transportation is made possible, coking is done in all household, and heating and cooling in some region of the world, and lastly, one of the most significant part, electricity!

Also, the production of energy is closely connected with the modern style of living including economic growth, population growth, water use, and the use of goods and services.

However, this joy is progressively being short-lived as the use and production of energy are boosting climate change. For example, in the U.S. alone, the method and manufacture of power are responsible for more than 80% of U.S. greenhouse gas Emissions.

Furthermore, the changes felt in the temperature, sea level, the severity, and frequency of event emanating from climate change is hitting the amount of energy produced and delivered in the U.S., and all around the world. And this isn't meaning well for the globe.

Climate change is expected to take a toll on all energy system. Therefore, there will be a change in the demand for cooling and heating facilities. Also, there will be a change in the differences in the solar, hydro-power and wind resources. More impact will be felt on thermo-electric power structures.

All these impacts and several other physical impacts will negatively impact reliability, the price and different impact hitting the energy supply to the environment. Other effects may be on an increased used of fossil fuels, or more money will be invested in energy infrastructure that will eventually bring about an increase in greenhouse gas emissions.

Take, for example, the impact that it will have on the efficiency on the power supply. There might be a reduction in the power stations. Another aspect of renewable energy will be influenced too. Recall that there has been a move to decarbonize the energy sector, but this adverse effect will undermine the process and success.

To ensure that mitigation techniques are adopted at its peak, there must be several incredible strategies to be executed.

The hydropower generation, as a result of an increase in temperature and the alteration of precipitation patterns, there will be little effect on the overall global resources. Although, more precipitation will increase the potential for electrical production. But increased drought in the Nordic region halts this provision. Further, the increasing wind speed is a green light for the productivity of electricity that will be generated from wind turbines, but in storming areas, wind turbines will be completely turned off to ensure that more damage is not caused to the facility and residents.

More point to consider is that the use of energy has influenced the earth atmosphere; the system that has previously been used in generating is being disrupted. Also, a shutdown of power plants in New England due to drought -from hot weather, there are restrictions placed on some companies because they didn't have access to abundant water. Sadly, that type of problem is expected to go on the rise.

More and more solutions are being sought. For example, several experts are suggesting that there should be a power upgrade, that is to modernize how it is being operated. This technology will be used to limit the risk of damages done. Although, some facilities are buried underground to reduce their impact. Sadly, flooding came, washed and disrupt some of the facilities that are buried underground. Others even understand that there is much research that will be done to limit the use of fresh water for the generation of power.

131

In the European region too, there are several hits of climate change in their energy sector. Thus, their challenge to increase the use has been in existence. Well, they are set for the race too - combating the impact and seeking for a more improved way of generating power or energy in a way that influence will not be much.

Well, this chapter is immensely to not only explain the problem climate change bring to the energy sector, but it will feature the best and most recent attempt to restore and cut the losses.

In the aspect of energy demand and supply, you will have to see how climate change has impacted the increase in the market for power and the decrease in the amount. Also, you will see the link between the availability of water and the need for energy. Also, storm increase and storm surge would have a comprehensive look. You will see wind speed and renewable energy.

Indeed, climate change has placed electricity at high risk. But is it something you have to worry about? Will it have a permanent impact or temporary impact? Also, there has been the development of renewables. How has it been increased? What are they? And how have they been of benefit to the globe and energy sector as a whole?

I've provided clarified answers to these questions, thus if there is any question you are passionate about seeing the response to, relax, read and get your answers. But, to start with, let's start from the first keen part: the impact on demand and supply of energy.

## Energy Demand and Energy Supply

Climate change will undoubtedly impact energy supply and demand, but the answer worth asking is "to what extent?" The issue of climate change influencing energy is one of the top agendas for policymakers across the globe. And the reason is solely to drive the growth of the economy in a country; energy is highly needed.

When we talk about the demand and supply of energy, what it entails is the act of generating, transmission and dispensing of power, specifically, electricity. Even though there are resources that are in abundance in creating different forms of energy over the world, the supply of energy is insufficient to meet the growing demand for electricity as the population increases. Climate change has been marked as the leading culprit in this drawback, even though there are human-made activities that are impacting it as well.

Recently, there are areas in some African Country that have been experiencing what is now known as "seasonal drought." Also, some areas have also undergone, undergoing excessive flooding. This is a clear indication of the threat to energy supply and corresponding demand.

Temperature is having the most impact on energy demand and energy supply. They will increase the demand and render an alteration on how it is being delivered and dependable.

In the Americans, where there exists a warmer climate will demand more electricity for the effective use of air conditioning. And then there will be limited natural wood, oil, and gas for generating heat. Also, if the country's climate increase by 1.8degree F, this will impact the rise in energy that will be adopted in cooling from the about 3-20%, then in sharp contrast, the demand for heating will decrease from about 4-15%. Generally speaking, in the U.S., the need for heating would require the reduction of significant parts of the Northern states, while in the southern U.S., only cooling demand will have an increase.

As this report shows, demand for electricity for cooling is likely to increase since the temperature will experience an increase and coupled with an extreme weather event, balancing up will be a problem. Therefore, this would bring about a deviation from the natural gas and oil from fuel to generate heat to be used for air conditioning.

And this deviation will bring about a problem; greenhouse gas emissions. However, the overall effect will be dependent on the energy source utilized. Including alternatives adopted.

Further, the apex electricity demand during summer time tends to increase in nearly all regions in the United States. Balancing up this high demand will result in generating new energy. Also, formal strategies of managing will go extinct, while there will be a new invention of new approaches or management policies, these new models will cost more money, since it's new, acquiring it may be more expensive compared to the one used and is not meeting up with current demand. So, the energy section should be ready to part with at least hundreds of billions of dollars in investing in this new generation model.

Although presently, there is the existence of some fossil fuel and nuclear power plants, there might be a problem of inefficiency due warming of the climate, and these fossil fuel and nuclear power plant make use of water for cooling. What happens if the rain expected to be cool, becomes hotter? In a sense, when the water gets cooler, more efficiently, the power plant will function, but in a situation where the water gets hotter, the inefficiency will no doubt occur.

Additionally, although the demand of electricity will keep growing, scientific reports and updated research have shown that climate change will pose a significant wreck on not just the supply alone, but ensuring that the amount is clean, affordable and sustainable. And when these three factors are lacking, the masses suffer. This will happen since there will be an increase in extreme weather like temperature, fluctuating rainfall, and other results of climate change. As mentioned above, they impact the infrastructure built and also affect the ability to generate energy via thermal and hydro means.

To drive home the point further, take a closer look at what happened in the Gulf of Mexico where Hurricane Katrina strikes. The disaster as a result of climate change had an impact on the U.S. energy sector. How? The event disabled a more substantial part of the U.S. oil and gas production, and it alters the accurate processing of those energies. The impact needs critical analyses though since in eradicating the problem, power will also be the need.

Interestingly, governments of the world have been made to sit, discuss how to redesign the structure of the global energy system, the distribution pattern and how to maintain that energy is secured. While the U.S.

government were assessing the impact of climate change on the energy sector, they were able to see the most common effect that is impacting the energy sector: water temperature, increase in air, decrease in water availability in some regions, storm surge.

In overall analyses, the most frequently analyzed is the demand and supply of energy. The request caters for the climate change impact on the use of power, the amount, in turn, examines how climate change impacts the production, the transmission, and distribution of energy.

Conclusively on this, the impact of climate change on energy demand and supply is that much work needs to be done to ensure the practical application and supply of energy. But it should be noted that the success of each country will be dependent on the nature of the energy sector. So, I strongly feel there should be a global standard that will be introduced and which every state must align with. Also, there should be more scrutiny on how an individual's state manages their energy system. If the issue of energy demand and supply can be checkmated in the grassroots, the whole will have a tremendous benefit.

Apart from the temperature that impacts energy supply and demand. Water availability also has a role to play, and what are the positions? What is the recent development regarding the solution to the impact? Let's have a look at that in the preceding paragraphs.

### Water Availability and Energy

When it comes to energy and water, they are closely related. And this is seen in what water is used in accomplishing. Additionally, power is required to ensure the more availability of water, for many uses which is including and not limited to treatment, desalination. For instance, to transport water from one region to another, energy is needed, to pump and supply either large or small community, energy is also required, in treating drinkable water and waste-water, energy is also required. On the other hand, to run, efficiently many power plants, just getting clean water isn't sufficient and enough. It has to be cool! No wonder in the United States, hydroelectricity is a vital source of power/energy.

Energy is highly useful for water management and several modern developments. As said above, it is like a chain; water infrastructure is dependent on groundwater extraction, distillation, waste-water management, transportation, treatment, and purification. Thus, in the operational cost of water, energy is vital.

How the effect of water availability is related to the energy is when there is an alteration in precipitation, where there is high increase in drought and the snowpack suffers a tremendous reduction and when the timing of snow melting changes. Let's get closer to figures and statistics that prove this to be real and valid.

For example, in today's withdrawal, more than 15% of global water is used in meeting energy production. And sadly, these waters are not even sufficient for the world's use. Besides, irrigation water that is globally targeted for biofuel production is estimated at 2% of all irrigation water.

For example, power plants demand a large amount of water to cool. And as estimated, on an average, just an hour kilowatt of electricity use will require approximately 96 liters of water be taken from lakes or open river. But is the power plant getting that at a sufficient rate? In the southeast and west, there is growing competition for the need of water to meet their demand, in the face of increasing competition and the growth in the economy and more effort is placed to assure that the natural ecosystem is maintained.

Additionally, there are several local governments in these areas that have rather than intensifying their effort in developing new power plants; they reduced their pacing. And the reason for their action isn't tricky to grasps. This is because generating a new power plant will demand extraction of water furthermore, and presently there isn't sufficient cooling water to cool the power plants that are running.

Heat is also playing its part apart from irregular precipitation. The increase in the intense heat will increase how electricity is being demanded. Accordingly, this undeniably will have an immense effect on the water available for use in the region severely affected by weather. To add to the point, recall that when there is an increase in temperature, there will be an increase in evaporation which will also reduce the abundance of water. All these will lead to much stress on water. Apart from the southeast and southwest region, other regions are feeling the effects of climate change, and it is impacting their energy supply and water stress. Another factor that will also stress water availability is the adoption of growing crops for biofuel energy and biomass.

Nevertheless, the impact is based on the type of crops that are being grown, how agriculture is being practiced, and the management method of water and nutrient management. Even though other several factors are impacting this region, there is a green light that points on how it stresses water resources. Well, in this regard more policy should be adopted to ensure strict management of both agriculture and water management.

Another aspect that shows the link between climate change and energy is the volume and the perfect timing stream flow. And you see, among all components that are sensitive to the timing and amount of stream flows, hydroelectric power plants are found in this category. In some countries especially, when they experience a rise in rainfall, those who manage the dams will release some water - I've practically experienced that. This is done so that flooding could be prevented from affecting electric turbines. However, this could mean ill for some life in the water. For example, ensuring that stream flows for the sake of hydroelectric dams is maintained could lead to an effect on salmon habitat.

If more water will be needed for irrigation and drinking, will they be sufficient? It's a doubt! Because the impact of an increase in temperature and evaporation will add to the energy demanded in the provision of quality drinkable water and irrigation supply. And look at it, when you don't have much water needed for drinking, and you still need more water to improve the efficiency of water provided. See the problem? For instance, in the ensuring of quality fresh water, more energy is required to ensure that the desalination plants will exceedingly do a conversion of water to clean water.

Summarily, you would have seen how closely interwoven energy and water availability is. On the one hand, we need water for more electricity efficiency and distribution, and on the other hand, more power to generate more water. But climate change is serving as a pit; we need to bridge the gap! It is necessary and essential!

Remember, that in the recent study in the United States, I mentioned sea level rise and storm surge as one of the most significant impacts on energy. There is a convincing point below that buttress the point in the succeeding paragraphs.

## Sea Level Rise and Storm Surge

I've decided to use more data and statistics in the United States in buttressing the point deeper. In case you are wondering why this is so, the reason is that the more significant portion of U.S. energy facilities is situated in the coastal area and as a result of the establishment, their sensitivity to sea level rise and storm surge is large and high. Indeed, other regions with this type using this strategy will have a close if not similar hit by sea rise and storm surge.

Consequently, transmission lines and generations of electricity will be placed on high risk in the coastal region. The fuel port is not excluded from this threat.

The sea rise and storm surge come as a result of changes in the extremity and frequency of events-climate change! These events will damage any facility that is either erected around the region and will go a long way in shortening the energy required to drive the economy better, and it is expected to have a bearing on the lives of people. Substantiating this, will real events will be so awesome? You can check it out below.

In the Gulf of Mexico where the U.S. energy infrastructure is located. Something worth considering is happening. So many coastal plants erected, as the sea level rise in that region, they are now less than three feet above sea level. That is a high susceptibility to damage shortly. There would be more Hurricanes in coastal areas which would lead to an increase in the alteration of the supply of energy. Globally, there should

138

be more effort to bring about the impact of sea level rise in the coastal region and how to combat it.

Sadly, the continual increase will also lead to many oil drilling platforms to be vulnerable to more attack of extreme weather. In a 2005 extreme event that hits the coastal region, Hurricanes Katrina and Rita have wrecking damage on more than 100 platforms. Additionally, it has led to damaged pipelines. With what astounding impact? More markets even in the developed land, New York and England are impacted.

Lines and electricity distribution will be impacted by flooding too. Yes, they have the tenancy to wreak havoc. If after an extreme event like sea rise and storm surge and flooding arises, even if the government of the region attempts to restore the problem, there is going to be a glitch. The issue will impact on the repair work that would want to be executed by groups of experts, even if after that war has been fought, management becomes a significant issue. In the meantime, there will be an impact on power outages. But definitely, it will have a severe effect on the energy system.

Moreover, even though more effect would be expected on the facilities, the power outages that would result from disruptions of oil and gas pipeline will be more severe. The transportation facilities will feel the impact; they will need to transport more oil and coal. The effect will be as a result of severe storms and precipitation. They are likely to wash off the railway tracks. Not that alone, they will impact marine transportation that makes navigation highly tricky.

The way flooding attacks the energy system is high. It disables the cooling systems designed for power plants leading to more overheating and release of toxic compounds. In Japan, the power plant located in the region of Fukushima Daiichi was impacted by flooding as a result of the tsunami in 2011, many strict demands were made to power plants. Thus, there was the release of radioactivity which led to immediate evacuation of more than 45 million occupants.

The occurrence of flooding in the United States coastline is becoming much. For example, the US Environmental Protection Agency (EPA) has reported that more than 26 measured coastal regions have experienced a tremendous level of flooding since the 1950s. The rate, however, hasn't stopped; instead, they have been increasing in many locations.

As sea level rises, the related impact, storm surge must be considered. The magnitude and frequency of storm surge, however, have increased. In China, the Philippines, Korea, and Japan have all felt the destructive power of super typhoons. The intensity in the past four decades has increased from 12% to 15%.

In the future, there are many projects of power plants, and if the condition does not recede, they will still be impacted. Just because changes are expected to be fast, they are faster than thought. Just like the government would fight all another impact of climate change, more strategies must be put in place so that they can comfortably win the war in all regions.

Many solutions may have been suggested. At least in California, there are suggestions for Levees and Seawalls, a massive dike under the golden gate bridge, elevated development, floating development, developing structures that will be able to handle flooding or in a better way capture the stormwater, living shorelines, better handling of managing retreats. As experts reveal, there are only a few potentials from all these strategies, and it would lead to another problem even if it will solve the problem temporary.

Take, for example, the strategies of managed retreat in the neglected area close to the shoreline. This strategy has been regarded as a political quag! It would demand more legal and several other issues. And that is because not all people will be interested in selling their properties. For some areas, shoreline communities, they would be unable to adapt. Moreso, retreating might result in more costs that are going to be so higher than relocation or cleaning up the environment. If at all, there will need to remove toxic off the situation.

With this mentioned point, there is more need to develop new strategies that will have limited or nearly no significant impact. Now it is high time to elucidate on how massive and significant the impact on wind speed and renewable on energy.

## Wind Speed and Renewable Energy

You might hurriedly think that wind energy is a form of renewable energy and as such should there be a real concern about it? It is good we find out. And that is accurately what I am bent on accomplishing. I'll be using Europe as a case study, after that, I'll be revealing figures that are available, from the United States, United Kingdom, the Mediterranean, West Africa, to reinforce the point further.

Well, just like every other aspect related to energy generation, climate change will have a high impact on wind energy production. One of the latest research available is the one carried out in Europe and will be used in ensuring that the idea is well tailored. Europe is a focal point here because they have a big challenge for wind energy.

In Europe, the average wind power production of all the continent will have a little change by the end of the 21st century. Nevertheless, there will be extreme seasonal fluctuations and drastically reduced low wind are been expected to take rise, that is, to happen! Additionally, in Europe, today, electricity generated from renewable sources is a contributory factor to the supply of energy, however, while the power is being transmitted, at least from the production center and the grassroots, where it is needed.

Further, wind energy has shown potential as a renewable energy source. But as at present it is affected by an extreme weather event, there are firm conclusions that it will lead to fluctuations and rapid climate change. There is more to the study done by researchers. Regarding their research, there are some models generated that are placed on simulation on the actual and real European climate condition. To ensure a more accurate precision of wind energy production on the area, spatial resolution is 12 kilometers, and the temporary resolutions adopted is 3 hours, exactly 180 minutes. Besides, there is an assumption that a wind plant of height above 100m is taken in the simulation.

After the analyzation, the results aren't awe-inspiring. For example, the average wind power that will be produced would have only a small difference at the tail end of the 21st century. The range, however, is expected to hit the differences between plus or minus 5%. Well, in some centuries, the report shows that much higher wind may be expected to get an increase of 20%. All these two changes are as a result of climate change.

Regional wise, the study shows some variations, for example in the northern, eastern and central Europe from daily usage to time scales. Then wind power meeting it's optimal stage will not happen frequently; that is, it will be something that will happen just once in a while.

Furthermore, it is projected that wind farms would even be used harnessing climate change, but countering the plan, warming that result from climate change will drastically reduce the power that wind can generate both in the UK, Mediterranean and in the US in line with latest research and development.

Although, in the past decades, wind farms have proven to be a substantial way of addressing the impact of climate change, and gladly, they have reduced carbon emission significantly. But sadly, it has been researched that this power is set to drop in the future. The research has seen some significant changes in the way wind power operates.

However, that d0oes not suggest that investing in the form of energy should be prohibited. But what it means is that in the future planning of wind energy, this knowledge should be taken into consideration. And more importantly, more prospect of wind energy limiting carbon emission should also be investigated.

Also, Japan is to suffers from the impact of climate change on wind energy. Japan wind farm is expected to have a fall by 58kW. However, this is because of the effects of climate change on wind energy. In the U.S. there will be a drop too, about 49kW. And the U.K which is expected to be at the lowest decline among these three parts would have a reduction of about 36kW.

notwithstanding, in regions like Australia, there is speculation that if warming goes higher, there will be an increase in the future. This is because in this region, the wind is targeted to be higher, some west African countries will have an improvement too. The reason why coastal area will have an increase in wind energy is that the warming that is happening in the land is faster than the one occurring in the ocean. That different is identified as the energy means for those winds. So, understandably, the more it warms in that region, the more the increase in the wind power will be felt.

Conclusively, we can fight climate change, even in the wind sector. Even though some government is not keen about our environment, with collective efforts, we can attain this height of change. It is also right that everyone makes it a point of duty to report any ill use of the environment that will not only lead to an increase in the carbon emission but will additionally threaten the alternative, that is, the renewable energy suggested to help win the war.

But, apart from all these impacts explained above, a skeptic mind may want to know if these are just the ways climate change impact the energy. Unfortunately, there are more. Sadly, these two that will be discussed below are so devastating that it is mandatory that we make changes as faster as we can.

## Ways Climate Change Puts Electricity at High Risk

From all that has been emphasized on, from the impact of climate change on energy demand and supply, water availability, storm surge, and sea level rise, there are more high risk that is bent on facing the global energy sector in the future to come, we must be prepared for this ill effect and ensure that all preparation to combat it are of significant value, and would work.

Even though there is a projected solution that I'm sure if adopted over time, there will be a tremendous impact, positive impact on our electricity system, globally. But before I start on revealing to you these ways, examine the threat that befalls the world if nothing is done! That will reinforce seriousness in many, and then they will be keen on making changes.

Indeed, our electricity system is susceptible to all extreme events - which the major ones have been discussed, but in the years ahead, there are about 75% assurance that it will increase if they're less effort.

According to current statistics, from the period of 2011 to 2012, just a year, more than 25 extreme weather disaster brings many damages, for example, more than 1000 infrastructures costing more than $188 billion were damaged. As if that was not enough, consequently, in the year 2012, this action led to the loss of energy use. At least, more than 8 million individuals were deprived access to electricity across 21 states due to the strike of Hurricane Sandy.

Let's discuss two of the high risk, since the issue of sea level rise, water and temperature has been extensively discussed. These two, wildfire, and heat waves will wreck much of the highest impact.

1. ***What Damaging Effect Wildfire Would Have on Electricity System.*** You can see that among the climate change impact hitting the energy sector discussed, must of them would not bring permanent damage, what do I mean? Take, for example, the issue of water availability, this wouldn't lead to complete loss of facilities, it can only displace them, and when the area is cleaned up, some of it might be recovered and reused. But can the same thing be said on wildfire? Absolutely no!

Immediately, a wildfire would destroy transmission poles, infrastructures built or erected, which will burn them entirely and condemn those facilities utterly, if lives are lost during the event, that would be more devastating! Now let me ask you, do you think, all these can be restored? They will have to purchase another facility since wildfire will devoid them of re-use. If some of the officials died in the event, a new set of employers would be employed, trained and before

144

they could adapt into the system, it would take more time, and this will affect those in need of electricity for their daily running. But is that all? Sadly, there is still more!

The burning of cables, lines and other electrical utilities will lead to release of smokes and other particulate matters. These matters will be toxic to health even electrical facilities. These particulate matters have the power to ionize the air, develop an electrical route that's far away from transmission lines, and finally to lead to the complete shutdown of the tracks.

With these, wildfires have multiple impacts extending beyond the complete damage of facility to human lives too. Unfortunately, the increasing occurrence of fire is alarming, using the U.S. as a case study, the existence of lights in the 1980s was just 140 in number, but in the year 2000 to 2012, it had increased to about 250 in number. Sincerely, this is sad! Millions of dollars are going down each time this incident occur.

  2. *More Frequent and Severe Heat Wave.* Heat waves have a part to play in the wrecking of havoc on the electricity system. One of them is decreasing the efficiency of the power supply. And this isn't just the right time where ability will suffer. And this is because the growing population is necessitating a better knowledge in the amount of power since the demand is high. In a bit to meet up with the market, as mentioned, more stress is added which in the long run might lead to damage of some or facilities. In North America, there are occurrences of more heat waves and this is devastating.

Generally, electrical systems need cooling air, not heat, but the impact of climate change makes the later what we battle with. It has now been seen that heat waves last more than three days now, during the last decades. In St. Louis for example, heat waves have been more occurring. For example, there have been continuous three-day heat waves than it was in the 1940s.

145

This has so much increased the number of humid days. There are hotter, dry days, faster in the Midwest. And to find the release from heat is highly harder because there are fewer cold days.

Ultimately, in the face of all these, even if there are strategies that are failing, more research should be done at the global level. And to achieve sustainable energy supply, and to ensure electricity supply are reliable, some many old-fashioned electricity structures need to be improved. Also, all the new systems should take into consideration all the impact of climate change. There should be significant ways to reduce carbon emission drastically because these are what are affecting the energy sector majorly, leading to temperature.

And that's why it is relevant to improve renewable energy as this offer the best way with less impact on the energy sector is because they will go a long way in making our power reliable and sufficient both in the short term or the long run.

As a result of that, there are better ways to improve renewable energy that I will like to feature in this chapter. I've taken time to detail the most reliable and resilient renewable energy since that is the best way to improve the electricity sector.

## Leveling Up Renewable Energy

It is true that renewable energy promises a solution to the impact of climate change, yet, there are more efforts to ensure that these renewable energy does not end up becoming one of the menaces we would start tackling again. Therefore, there should be ways to improve efficiency too so that there will be the creation of more resilient, reliable electricity system, I'll mention nine ways to improve this.

1. *It should be on a smaller scale, but with more distribution of energy.* If renewable energy like rooftop solar panel and wind turbines are made on a short range are distributed to a wide area there will be more benefit. For example, when extreme weather event happens, instead of affecting the large grid which will change a large number of people, only the area of renewable

energy will be damaged. And only those using that energy in that small scale will be affected.

This will extensively reduce the cost of repair of damage. And the smaller the replacement, the faster it will be.

2. *Limit the Risk of Water.* Undeniably, the amount of water needed for conventional power energy is high and will keep growing. Apart from the amount of water required, there will also be a need of water to cool the power and plant and going by what you've read so far, the availability of this is becoming so rear that the efficiency is suffering more. But when introducing any renewable energy, there should little or zero need for water for powering up.

For example, the use of solar panels and turbines does not require the use of water. This will reduce the stress on water resources and the growing demand with less supply. And again, the energy sector has less worry about the disaster that hits water resources.

3. *Using Low-Carbon Electricity.* One of the astounding benefits of renewable energy is an effort to reduce carbon emission. And that's an excellent way to solve the problem of carbon emission. You'd recall that the use of conventional electricity discharges more carbon emission into the atmosphere.

Gladly, using renewable energy will go a greater length in curbing this discharge of carbon emission. At every level, the use of this renewable energy should be made available in every country so they can have access to it and make good use of it.

4. *Adapting to Unavoidable Havoc of Climate Change.* We can't avert some of the consequences of climate change. To prepare the masses ahead of the impacts, they must be prepared ahead of this havoc. Some of the preparation to be adopted is buying more transmission lines, relocating some equipment to areas where there is the likelihood of climate change impact.

This can help to reduce the longer time of power outages, although these steps might not be excellent for long term use because it will be expensive. But for a short-term goal, it is a unique and dependable way.

5. ***Limiting the Demand Will Lessen Some Problem.*** Any home that embraces energy efficiency will reduce the demand for electricity from the power sector. Thus, instead of building more power plant to cater for the application, there wouldn't be a need, when there are fewer facilities, when disaster strike, there will be less impact on the facilities since only fewer facilities will be impacted.

Less impacted facilities would mean less cost of repairing the damage or even purchasing more equipment. And that will go along the way to disburse money into more profitable investments.

6. ***Susceptibility Assessment.*** It is one thing to know that a location can be impacted; it is another to note the level of impact that can be done. To validate this governments should prioritize on conducting this test that will show how each country and city or town is susceptible.

It will also help in knowing actually how the impact will be on the electrical facilities, and other structures built. Then if there will be any measure to take to avoid or prepare ahead. This will also help in revealing the extent of damage they can expect, and it can foster proper planning and prevent excessive spending or spending on what will later not be used or utilize.

7. ***Upgrade Electricity Facilities.*** Honestly, many electrical utilities need an upgrade. Power plant operators should do research that will use less water in powering up their facilities, thus reducing the dependability on water.

Moreover, there are other flexible ways that power plants operators can incorporate into their planning. Some of the ideas are adopting microgrids that can isolate outages to some locations. And yes, they can expand transmissions. And to accomplish this, there should be more research and technological inventions.

8. ***Boost Clean Energy Policies.*** There is no better time to accomplish this than now. From the state and federal level, policymakers should support the notable inclusion of renewable energy.

Not that alone, they should also insist on expanding it so that more house can utilize it efficiently. The U.S. EPA should be swift about their implementation of standards, high standards that will trap more emission and introduce better alternatives.

9. ***Incorporate mitigation and Adaptability into Utility Planning.*** For proper adaptability and reduction, states and locals can inquire to know precisely how much will be needed to adapt and mitigate to the havoc of climate change.

Resilience, which will be discussed in chapter nine is also a great way to attack this issue.

If all these adopted, no doubt, renewable energy will be efficient and there will be less impact of climate change on the energy sector. However, researchers have shown that reducing carbon footprint will be of an immense boost to energy use and support the electricity system and the world as a whole. But the question I'll like to ask you is: "do you have an idea on how to go about it?" Relax, I've researched into 20 best and practical ways to accomplish that goal; they are explained below

## Other Ways to Enhance the Electricity System

As explained in the preceding paragraphs, the most practical ways to reduce your carbon footprint print is what will be gaining our attention. Be informed that the Union of Concerned Scientists researched these ways.

Also, other options that will be featured are going to encourage companies to reduce carbon emissions and how they can go about it.

Furthermore, I'm aware that more people, probably including you are interested in knowing how swift the options will work out. It does gladden my heart to tell you that some, at least the first two, will give result in minutes. Yes, as the end, you will see how it has become everyone's goal.

*1. Switch to Renewable Energy.* Yes! Even though more has been said on renewable energy, making it the first option should instill in you how vital and essential it is to incorporate that in your home. So, if that's not what you are using now, make a move and start using it. You can gain access via your utility provider or via a renowned and valid renewable energy provider. The bottom line: "You have to switch to renewable energy."

*2. Calculate Your Carbon Footprint.* This shouldn't feel like a Herculean task to you. And if feel it is, this is why I said it shouldn't. There is technology made available today that can relieve you the burden, they would make the calculation, or as an alternative, you can purchase carbon offset from a reliable and certified seller. The highest carbon emission comes from transportation, and the closest is the stuff you are buying. Now if you have a similar trend reduce it immediately.

*3. Limit Driving.* Since one of the highest emission carbons comes from driving, if you own a car, develop a strategy that will help reduce it instantly. How? You can turn to using bike, and you can invest in carpooling or use public transport as an alternative. Another alternative would include trekking down to your place of work, where you want to make a purchase, visit a friend or family member within the proximity of 2 miles to your house. Even though the primary goal is reducing the carbon emission, you benefit from reduced cost from running and maintenance expenses

*4. Do Some Research.* It takes time to do research though, yet, it makes a significant gain to do that. Your inquiry will be focused on how to be energy efficient in a larger scale, which is the most excellent way that will make much impact. The study could be more on your home, the equipment, and electrical appliances to purchase that will reduce energy use and cars that have low emissions of carbon. And just like a growing trend, some are feeling more attached to a more car-free system, and with more rise, the fight can be won leading to drastic reduction.

**5. *Limit Purchase of New Products.*** There are so many resource-intensive products that emit a large amount of carbon into the atmosphere. They are mostly heavy and highly packed. Instead of spending hell of money purchasing these items, other substitutes can be used rather than buying more new products.

**6. *Be a minimalist.*** A minimalist lifestyle is an excellent way to reduce utility consumption. Its time you de-clutter your pieces of stuff and then limit some facilities that consume more electrical utility. Although, having the right attitude toward minimalism is good. For example, you apply the lifestyle of minimalism in your home to work, and nearly all you do. Just be critical about your needs and see those you need to away with.

**7. *Reduce Energy Use.*** Your orientation and focus should be more on reducing energy use. To embark on that journey, be keen only on buying more energy efficient unit like heating, cooling and water heating. You can even proceed to seal the cooling and heating duct that you make use of in your home. Cultivate the habit of maintenance, add insulation, limit the use of stoves, limit standby energy consumption, always be conscious of your light and appliance when leaving home and going to bed, and finally, for better output, get an energy audit.

**8. *Turn to Locally sourced Material.*** Instead of buying processed materials, resort to buying unprocessed one — for example, an unprocessed meal from local farmers. You can also buy food from restaurants that invest in a green environment. Also, to avoid food waste, make adequate planning that will make you cook just what it isn't needed. And you can freeze whatever excess you later have. It is better you microwave instead of having to prepare another meal that will require more energy and impact on energy generated.

**9. *Limit Your Water Use*.** In generating electricity, much water is needed, and if at all home, there is less use of water, then we can have sufficient water to power plants. Also, another critical point to note is that when water is being pumped for used in any household, more power supply is needed. Thus, in addressing this issue, I'll advise you to buy a tap, shower heads, and washing machines and dishwashers that utilizes little water. Also, if you see any leaky faucets, you should get to address it instantly. Since a drought can lead to evaporation of water, you should purchase pipes that are resistant to heat and drought.

**10. Be Supportive.** Undeniably, some organizations foster the idea of being energy efficient. They are bent on educating women and girls. This move is to bring stability in our population so that there won't be a drastic jump in the community, thus increasing population. These organizations are spread across the whole world. Make an inquiry to see the one closer to you, and when you find one to be of support to the person. And the truth is that those organizations need more voice and need more people than will enhance their publicity.

**11. *Embrace the Attitude of Recycling*.** How good are you at recycling? Maybe you don't? If you are good at recycling, then, keep it up and always seek more ways to do better. But if you haven't, imbibe it in your everyday activities. When traveling, only buy products that can be recycled. There are several regulations and laws governing the recycling of products and material, thus research online on how it is being done and the type of materials that you can purchase in your country that will be recycled. Recycling limits the amount of energy used in producing another entirely new product that will cost more time and energy.

**12. *Compost Your Food Waste*.** Do you know what it means to compost food waste? One of the reasons why you don't know how to go about it is because some cities have issues getting it right. It is even accurate to ensure that you create a home food waste plan that you will be strict with. You can store food waste in a plastic container. An additional move is that you can dig a ground to pour waste, you can feed livestock, you can also buy composters that will help with the correct way of composting.

13. *Limit Flights.* Plan your traveling with wisdom. Even if it is within your means, be reminded of the carbon emission that will be emitted when you fly, they will still be of adverse effect on the energy sector. In addition to limiting the impact your use of the airplane, you can request for carbon offset. You can be more precise. And this is how: when buying, there is an option identified as "individual" pick it and then when you see the airplane icon, click on it, you will see the airplane calculator.

*14. Install Solar Panels in Your Home.* A solar panel converts solar energy to electrical energy, and that reduces the use of electricity generated from plants. Since it's a natural power, you cut the emitting of carbon energy. For more efficiency, you can dedicate some of the energy from solar to some of the small but regularly used electrical facilities like bulbs, fans, and chargers. This will reduce the stress of the emission of carbons. Neighbors around might want to imitate you-you can tell people about the benefits derived from it, and all together you can reduce carbon emission.

*15. Invest in Energy- Intensive Exercises.* We know how healthy exercising is, but what is the idea of exercising and still impacting another adverse effect into the society. It will amount to nothing other than running on a slippery ground where one is susceptible to dying or being severely injured from sliding. Therefore, to have the best exercise, use energy-intensive ones like hiking, as against sky diving. And other options that require less energy. Most tourists have even related how enjoyable it will be to hike alongside other tourists than sky diving that might have more risk.

*16. Lodge Only in Green Hotels.* This is the right time to teach some companies and organizations that this is time to invest in green energy. And we can teach them by reducing how we are using their facility. Take for examples there are many green hotels now that have been complying with the effort of reducing carbon emission. However, some are only turning away to that approach. The way we can teach this one is limiting how we use their facility. Therefore, when you travel, first inquire for a hotel facility that uses green energy.

*17. Climate Action Needs Support.* Are you willing to support climate action? Please be ready. Just like you'd when next you will be lodging in a hotel. The same thing should be extended to companies and firms that sell products and services to their customers. Investigate into the companies and check to see if they are utilizing or embracing actions that show they are in support of curbing the impact of climate change, then purchase from them, but if at any they are not ready don't buy from them. You can encourage people to take that bold step too. Taking these actions will force these companies to take measures.

*18. Support a Candidate That Have Climate Action at Heart.* During manifesto and debate, a candidate running for an election will at that time reveal their interest and shows how they intend to bring relives to the masses. Pay attention to their speeches; whoever shows so much interest in limiting carbon emission would be interested in a better health community. Additionally, check into what they've personally done in recent times to ensure that they practice what they are advocating so that it wouldn't just be a strategy to get the position and do nothing after the must have gained power.

*19. Learn More Every day.* One of the reasons you purchase this book might be to educate yourself or for research purpose, or any other reasons outside this, it's wise move to educate oneself. But you can still educate yourself the more. You can keep track with WHO (World Health Organizations) or other Climate concerned organization that will without let-up will keep advising on how best to live with the impact of climate change or how to adopt. Also, there is a firm that converges people where ideas can be shared, and the latest development will be brought into the limelight.

***20. Be an Encouragement to the greenhouse.*** Finally! You won't just encourage by telling people, but you must practice it. Join a program that is solely based on how to practice this.

And there you go! The twenty (20) alternative ways to ensure a more efficient electricity system. And imagine how significant the result will be if everyone in every land practice this? Regardless of what some individual would think or would do, the action begins with you.

And to be honest with yourself, the knowledge you've gained from this intensive reading has helped reinforced your conviction to be more energy efficient. If they too can gain more understanding, they might want to be greener.

Have you been noticing that there have been changes in our seasons too? Some are coming faster, and some are good faster. There is so much imbalance. To what extent? How would you pick a climate goal change facing the shifting in seasons? These answers have been correctly provided in the next chapter. Not that alone, there is so much to be learned in the next chapter as it will lay a groundwork for the ways we can fight climate change in all facets of your life.

**Chapter Seven**

# The Effects of Climate Change on Seasons

## Shifting Seasons

Many centuries ago, the season was a subject of central focus for many. There are varying mistaken ideas about it. Most of these are affected by religious, superstitious and cultural believes. In actuality, more farmers back then offer prayer to the gods, they do so to get good harvests, rain and other aspects that would bring about huge yield.

But as science comes to the limelight, many of these believe start to fade. Peoples' access to scientific data that dispense the facts are noteworthy to some people and with the use of their window, at least, and the purchase of newspaper they can come to a reasonable conclusion. Sadly, this isn't for everyone! How about you? Do you see the season from the scientist's perspective?

Season, as defined from an astronomical perspective, they are represented by the northern or southern hemisphere's nearness to the sun. In the United States, for example, winter comes down as soon as the half of the planet slants slightly off the fireball. And for summer, it returns as soon as the Earth moves back in the direction of intensely hot plasma. This defines the reason why Alaska is known as the summer in Australia. Simply put, when the northern hemisphere moves off the sun, the southern on the other hand moves closer, and inversely.

Well, when it comes to the shifting of the season, if you aren't aware that the seasons are shifting, you are not alone! Many with busy schedules are oblivious about this. Some farmers, although a few ones who are not observant of their working condition aren't on the know too. They definitely, just like anyone else notice changes in precipitation, the increase in heat and some other noticeable changes in the weather; these changes ultimately

156

impact their yield; they know! Even though the apparent differences in climate could be a culprit, but there is one misconception that those in the developing world have.

For those who are aware, it is so unfortunate that they lay the blame on the "gods." They popularly say: "the gods are vexing." I call this: "blaming the unknown." Yes, laying accusation on what is never to be blamed is absurd and not practical at all! It retards progress in fighting the menace, and it fosters superstitious beliefs, it nullifies scientific researches that would have helped in combating this, excellently and flawlessly.

For people like you, you deserve to be armed with the right information; you need to know what "shifting seasons" is, how to help it and eventually, how an individual can stop the continual shifting of the seasons.

It is not a gainsaying that seasons are shifting. For example, from the thorough research from science, it has been verified that spring is arriving sooner, winters, however, are becoming shorter, and even the freezing days that used to be abundant with time, that is, they are often longer, are becoming less, they are reducing.

Take for example, in research later published in the year 2009; the paper shows that in the year 1850 and 2008, there have been noticeable changes that have been felt. The hottest day of the year slides in sooner, precisely, it came nearly 48 hours earlier before their set date. And sadly, this trend has not gotten a halt. It's has grown more intense that if you notice, winter and summer are becoming more similar, that's not enough, spring is coming earlier every year, and for fall, it has disappeared.

As expected, those changes will have a bearing on the accurate timing of the life cycle. Such impacts would be felt on when pollinators will arrive and the blooming time of flowers. It influences the migration of some species and several other events.

These changes in the cycle will inevitably have an impact on the ecosystems. Is there going to be a difficulty in understanding why? Most species will have to respond differently to environmental indications. As a result, species that rely on each other will have to suffer the eventuality.

For some species that can identify the changes in the conditions, they often do better, and that is very reasonable! What they are echoing, in essence, is that: resources are available, this is the best time to produce leaf, this is the best time to flower. But for some species that aren't making any move and are waiting, they are gradually disappearing off the landscape.

Additionally, researchers have seen that the temperature that is averaged over any given year is experiencing a drastic increment. All that is responsible for the warming of some months than the other. Besides, over the land, the variation felt in the warming of one month to another is the result in the shift in the timing of the season, and the reduction in the disparity between the winter and summer temperature, which are all clear indications that the seasons are shifting. And recall as I have said earlier, some birds are migrating earlier, some plants are blooming sooner, and besides, mountain snow is melting sooner as well.

This timing and shifting that is happening alongside the rise in temperature have led to many experts thinking that human-activities is one of the leading effects of climate change and that is responsible for the shift. Nevertheless, there are more reasons tailored to this.

There are some winds identified as "Northern Annular Mode" that has been consistently changing over the same time range. Thus, it is investigated that a change in the direction and frequency of the wind can drive heat from the ocean right on the land, with an expansive effect on the timing of the season. They affirm that the link between these, wind pattern and the seasonal shift is not the only strong evidence that can be used in explaining the overall concept of the "shift."

Moreover, researchers have been looking into other possible causes like the great drying of the global soil, and this will lead to more heat on the surface of the land when it reacts to the rays of the sun, and the rate of energy absorbed by the atmosphere due to increased pollution from the industry. But no cause has been more evident than the one from climate change.

To conclude, this section would have helped you see in detail, how climate change, as the leading culprit, wreck impacts on the seasons. If at all you've been noticing the changes in the seasons, you've learned to channel the blame on the real culprit. Though not comfortable about the issue, but the knowledge brings us closer to solutions that are long-lasting and would have a significant impact!

No doubt, you've understood what shifting seasons are, but how does it operate? Indeed, you'd not get this aspect clearer without knowing how it works. As you read further, the next paragraph discusses how seasons shift broadly. It will even make the overall idea of shifting seasons come to live!

### How Seasons Are Shifting

The first thing you'd need to know that will aid your understanding of shifting seasons is what this aspect is directly linked to. As revealed, shifting seasons are directly related to global warming. And you'd remember that global warming is one of the results of drastic climate changing. Okay, let's proceed.

Further, global warming, makes the global temperature of the atmosphere becomes warmer. Then, when there exists a slight alteration in the heat, this will lead to moving the spring melting sooner, leading to a delay in the first thaw in the fall period. And you should know, that the atmosphere is so sophisticated that a slight change in the habitat will cut across all that exist therein.

Accordingly, several trees will be profoundly affected; then spring wildflowers will be led to bloom just so early than the norm. And that's not all.

The change will make winter shorter; then spring will appear so early. Then, it can be expected that summers will often be looking longer, then fall in turn, will come later. The bloom dates and leaf are often effective and useful in indicating the change in climate, most times they are the signs we read.

Besides, more conviction has been reached by scientists worldwide that the sooner presence of springs is closely associated with current global warming that is happening in the global climate. Also, these alterations will have an impact on the ecosystems and world society at large.

The appearing of spring earlier than its usual time will lead to lengthier growing seasons, and there will be more sufficient-though detestable existence of pests and more invasive species - plants and animals. Additionally, there will be lengthier allergy seasons. How these are closely affected will weaken their adaptability. Also, more species would be more pushed out of existence from the invasive ones. Not that alone, more pests will mean more damage to the farming system.

Besides, the availability of warm weather presence in late winter can lead to what will be known or identified as "false spring." And all these triggers the new growth or development of plants to start coming up when it is not actual time. And when this happens, more susceptibility to frost is undeniable. This is just typical in the United States now.

Thus, what can be concluded is that shifting season is a result of climate change that brings about global warming, which will alter the seasons that are already existing moving their appearance and when they occur.

There is a direct and indirect impact of shifting seasons. But below I will highlight four direct implications of shifting seasons while in the subsequent subheading, I will highlight the indirect consequences of shifting seasons. These four directs impacts lead to an indirect effect on the world as a we all experience today.

*1. **Alteration in the Life-cycle**. When seasons appear at the right time when they are expected to, the life cycle of species continues undisturbed, and they will cause no disturbance. But since shifting seasons will have an impact when seasons appears. There will be a misalignment in the life cycle process. Species that solely depend on each other will have to suffer the outcome.*

*2. **Higher Frost Risk**. The shifting in seasons brings about high frost risk. But how precise? The earlier presence of warm temperatures would lead to several trees and flowers that will be blossoming earlier, thus susceptible to frost actions. However, not all plants have the same response to frost- they have more vulnerability than each other. Therefore, plants that have more weakness will have difficulty in bearing fruit. And in cases whereby they produced any seed, nut or fruit produced will be frost-affected plants. Feeding on them will not be a delighted endeavor. The increase in climate change will make the condition more occurring and rampant.*

*3. **High Level of Drought**. Since the timing of snow-thawing will be critically impacted, more drought is expected and inevitable. There will be the existence of a lengthy period of summer. Thus, more drought will be experienced. This undeniably will hit more animals, plants and even human.*

*4. **Planting Zones Are Shifting**. The shifting in seasons will in a broader way affect the zones where planting occurs. For example, it is currently happening that planting zones are moving to the farther north, leaving the already existed plain. This reduces food shortages in some areas and increases or stabilizes other regions.*

*5.**Pests and Diseases**. This isn't even about their impact on humans. This is more about how shifting seasons leads to their increase in population and letting them escape death. Pests and some diseases, as a result of the previous summer, they will eat and populate. Even, some species of pests will in the milder winters have an increase in population, thereby more of these pests will survive the more.*

These changes definitely, will open a way for other severe impacts - indirect impacts. These impacts are evidently not a good music to dance to but reading about them can place us in a position where we will be ready to work things out.

Happily, it would interest you to know that "Land Trusts" are working some realistic plans that will make the world experience a bit of reliving. They've adopted conservation goals and the building of several management objectives. Let me briefly discuss them.

*1.**Conservation Goals.** Land trusts is waking up to the shifting of seasons in multiple ways. There has been the inclusion of several plants diversity that will assist dramatically in the restoration plans. These will grant fauna opportunity to have access to food and provide them a suitable habitat to match up with the changes in the season.*

*Moreover, some of their efforts also include conservative planning that minimizes risks and increases resilience, top of it, they have shown willingness and supported the move to mitigate greenhouse gas emissions, as this is a way to reduce the impact of shifting seasons shortly. Also, amazingly, more conservation firms are, and non-profit organization is working tirelessly in connection with profit-organization in ensuring that response to the global challenge extends to the local levels.*

*2.**Building Resilience**. Resilience is understood rightly as the ability of a system to survive through an extreme event. One of the ways this can be brought close to how shifting seasons are* *being tackled is identifying the real problem and limiting the threats. To achieve that obviously, there will be a need for more management objectives. So, several ways have been analyzed. They have to assess vulnerability. This is going to bring them closer to the solution. They would create adaptive management procedure. These will assist them in implementing new information gotten. Continually, more strategies are being executed, and with massive implementation, there will be a record of success.*

*Although in the management procedure, there will be a need for several solutions to be brought forward since there is no almighty procedure that will fit all circumstances. As a result, new strategies will be used in several locations and it will be tested to see if it is suitable in bringing about a positive change.*

*As a result, this will call for more unity and require several researches that will be made to bring about new development, and in that way, technological tools will be highly effective.*

Undeniably, there is other persuasive evidence that climate change is impacting the seasons. The evidence is found in the troposphere. Thanks to improved science that have made data evident and available for the use of the public. This powerful and robust evidence is the next point worthy of discussion.

### Strong Evidence of Climate Change's Effect on Seasons

More than ever before, scientists are always on the move to bring humanity closer to facts to enable a well-grounded understanding of the planet earth. The research on the impact of climate change has been taken to the troposphere, a part which is the lowest level of the atmosphere. And they found an incredible detail, that is even termed "powerful evidence" that climate change is having an indisputable impact on the seasonal temperature. Now, all required from you is to read and educate yourself further.

The recent study publicized in the Science journal indicates that climate change has led to an increase in the contrast seen in between the summer and the winter temperature that has been experienced across both Eurasia and North America over the past forty years. Indeed, there's so much strong evidence. The event could be held accountable for the result of the summer temperature that is always warming so soon and rapidly than winter temperature.

More facts revealed also indicate that validated substantial human influence on Earth's Climate isn't limited to global means. Also, it affects both the 'local and seasonal changes" as indicated by another researcher. Besides, as asserted by a prominent scientist, most of the world's weather begins from the troposphere, which reveals that the seasonal temperature could be impacting the likelihood of extreme weather events, which examples of these are flooding and drought.

In the following subheading, we'll be checking areas like sky high, satellite sentinels, the human activities, and other weather concerns; this will further reveal the evidence presented by science.

### Sky High

In Europe for instance, some studies reveal that the first-emergence dates of a more significant number of 500 plants species show that the first day of spring has an increased length of six-eight days in the past thirty years! Nevertheless, validating the extent at which the impact of seasonal changes can be explained by climate change, as against the natural climate variability poses a setback.

Therefore, in measuring the impact of climate change in contrast to natural variability, the road they turn out to is identified as "attribution analysis."

This new study is the first that will be applied in making a detail investigation of seasonal change which could be influencing the annual temperature right in the troposphere.

Conclusively on this part, researchers note that "results reveal that attribution investigation with the changes in the seasonal cycle shows strong evidence for a substantial impact of human impact on Earth's climate."

## Satellite Sentinels

This being the second on board for consideration has made researchers analyze the atmospheric temperature data that are on record by satellites over more than thirty decades, a period of 1979 - 2016 throughout the winter and summer months. The data from the map discloses the difference between the summer and winter temperature as mean per decade, that the change has been felt across the world.

Precisely, on the map, there are dark red spots that show where the variations between the summer and winter temperature, and over those years they have grown larger. Otherwise, the white, blue, dark color on the map reveals where the variations have become smaller.

What can be concluded? The differences between summer and winter temperature have gotten an increase, drastically in the mid-latitude regions, and specifically in the northern hemisphere. But you may want to know why the situation is actually like that.

In these regions, atmospheric summers temperature is speedily and swiftly having an increase than the happening in the winter temperatures - This is why there have been changes in the two seasons, they have been increasingly growing larger.

Additionally, the northern hemisphere is having more summertime warming than the southern hemisphere since it has more lands. And the availability of land goes a long way to suggest that there will be the presence of ocean extracting fewer heats from the area. And eventually, to increase atmospheric warming, from climate change will exist.

165

Experimentally, countries that have been experiencing the most significant impact is in the region of Mongolia and eastern Russia. Also, areas of western and northeast US have been experimented to have been influenced too. Lastly, the province of Europe has even gotten an increase in the seasonal tropospheric cycle. When investigation travels to the region of the UK, only a small change is experimented.

Furthermore, the map has more reality to reveal. For example, on the eastern edges of both North America and Eurasia, it has been that they have a tremendous impact on climate change. When investigated more, what was revealed as the reason was that during the winter in these regions, warmer air is transported from east to west, and this has led to lighter winters along the western part. Well, alterations in temperature are often not significant because the area is not highly seasonal. Instead, the season is in most cases, described by rainfall rather than by temperature.

Also, more facts show that the disparity between summer and winter temperatures all over the pole has experienced a recess in the last forty years. And as shown, winter temperature is coming faster than summer temperatures.

Even in the Arctic, this winter warming is impacted too, though little. And this happens when the sea ice starts diminishing in the summer months. And when there exists just little sea ice, the ocean is forced to absorb more heat, and this is later discharged during the winter period.

In conclusion, previous research indicates that the availability of polar clouds in the stratosphere is playing a significant role. Nevertheless, the reason atmospheric winter warming is accelerating so speedily over the Antarctica is not very clear.

## Significant Human Activities

To have a more validated claim as to how human activity is impacting the weather change, researchers have compared the result they have at hand from the satellite and the climate models. This model covers a period of 1979 - 2016, and inclusive are natural factors that can have an impact on the tropospheric temperature, these natural influences include aerosols and volcanic eruption and others. In ensuring that the effects of human-caused climate change are put into consideration, there was an inclusion of business-as-usual discharge. What was the result?

Only simulations that have the impact of human of the changes in climates would have an accurately speculations of the mode of seasonal temperature change that is being recorded by the satellites.

The result of the observation shows that reality observation is closer to model simulations. Also, we can now convincingly assert that humans are

## Weather Concerns

Nevertheless, it is still not obvious how temperature changes in the troposphere region can have an impact and affect conditions at the land surface. In a sense, there is still much to be learned here. However, it has been suggested that the changes in the timing and the potential of severe weather impact could affect too.

Finally, this research has shown that the troposphere is capable of revealing to us climate changes since that location houses all our weather. So, in the coming future, there could be more revelations as to the impact of climate change on our season.

With this powerful evidence you've seen on the impact of climate change on the season, there are more impacts of seasons shifting, there are other plants and animals that have been affected by moving season, can you find any of these in your location? And if it is true, is there a solution that can be meted out and will be an extensive one. You are a paragraph closer to the answers!

## Impacts of Shifting Seasons

The winter and summer that are shifting in are impacting the presence of plants and animals; the flowering and leafing of plants and the migration of animal species are just a few of the several impacts that shifting seasons bring. Shifting seasons have been responsible for the destruction of harvest, and this will result in food scarcity. In fact, among these, there are severe sad consequences of shifting seasons.

Scientific observations in nearly 100 countries that are based explicitly on the shifting of the season have revealed how badly the effect is being felt on poor folks. Following the report was a warning that if nothing is done to the shifting season just like the overall impact of climate change, in the next 5 decades, most of the bloomy economics improvement will be gone, and rapidly, what will be known as "climate-related hunger" would be one of the significant battle the world will have to wrestle.

Some of the impacts of the shifting seasons explained by "Suffering the Science" are outlined below. These are:

1.**Intense Hunger:** When many farmers are being interviewed across fifteen countries of the world on how severely the season is shifting and how rains are becoming less and less, the result is not appealing. They found out that in the region of Bangladesh, Nicaragua and some other countries they can't apply the farming experience they've gained for decades or if at all they try implementing it, they end up combating failed harvest over failed harvest. So, in countries like this, the ability to provide sufficient food will be difficult, hence hunger.

2.**Agriculture.** The report laid concern on rice and maize, the world's most vital crops which billions of people depend on. This is precisely true in areas like Africa, Americans, and Asia. These countries mentioned are battling a high drop in yield. The worst part is that this even happens under slight climate change event; little wonder the drastic climate change happening is hitting them so bad. They made a forecast aside from massive drop being experienced now, by saying that the decline in yield is expected to hit 20% in the year 2020 - months from now. And in fact, the region of sub-Saharan Africa and India will have a bad hit. In a closer figure, the loss Africa is expected to experience is pegged at $2billion a year. Therefore, the shifting seasons is playing a significant part in agriculture.

**3.Health.** If agriculture is impacted, we should be ready to experience a change in human health. But shifting season has made disease like Malaria and dengue more apparent. This type of infections are once bounded geographically, but as season shifts, these diseases also creep into new areas, affecting a large number of people due to inability to battle the conditions; they lack health care facilities, modern knowledge and all these increase their vulnerability and increase their lack of immunity. Buttressing the point further, the shifting season has led to more than 150,000 deaths since the 1970s era. And sadly, the more significant parts of the stats come from the Asian countries.

**4. Employment.** The increase in temperature as a result of shifting seasons would make it highly unsuitable for many to work just the rate, they've been working on hot summer days. And if they insist on working, they should get ready for health implications. A more concern goes to workers that dwell on per hour job, they would mostly be affected, and that will have a bearing on the economy. Regions expected to have more intense instability are tropical areas like Delhi, areas like this should get ready for the loss of worker productivity, in nothing less than 30% loss. What a huge loss that would be!

**5.Water Availability.** The shifting season is having an extreme impact on water. Use either for energy, agriculture, or for domestic uses. Water supplies are scarce in cities which include Kathmandu and La Paz which their dependent is found on Himalayan and Andes glaciers, and these are losing out functions continually. And at this stage, where more populations are growing and increasing, the battle for water will increase and with shortages of water it is impossible to meet up, thus problem of water disappearance is set to arise.

**6.Disasters.** There is some disaster that is not natural but expected to be on the increase as time passes by. Wildfires and storm surge are supposed to be occurring three times more than the usual occurrence in the year 2030. Recall, that I made it more apparent that the insurance company alone lost billions of dollars as a result of this disaster hitting companies and individuals. This is a signal for people that have no access to insurance; if any of their properties are eaten up by disasters, they would have to endure great loss.

7. **Displacement.** Currently, shifting seasons have displaced a more significant number of people all over the world, say, an estimated figure of 26 million individual. Although the considerable hit is in developing countries like Vanuatu, Tuvalu and the Bay of Bengal which are island communities have been forced to relocate from where they once were.

Undoubtedly, the shifting season is leading to more poverty. Sadly, those who live below the poverty line, working more to make ends meet are the enormous hit from this. And with this several information you've gained access to, it has become more glaring. And unfortunately, I have even been told that the globe is highly expected to have an increase in the rate of warming, say about 2 degrees. And why this is so is because nearly all the politicians in today's world aren't resolved to reduce the amount of carbon emitted into the air daily.

If you reside in a developed country, this level of increase may be of fewer worries, but how about folks that stay in developing regions, it will mean a deadly blow as it is speculated that more than 660 million will be affected.

When Professor Diana Liverman was speaking on this impact, he maintained that if severe cuts are not made into the discharge of carbon, there will be more problems. There will be more vulnerable people. Dwellers in tropical regions, with the majority of humanity, will have a significant impact.

Several suggestions are being given to the world government. They suggested that more fund is disbursed into the system so that adaptability would be of help to the world and those that are already feeling the impact of water, air, and food will be relieved. More important cuts are the companies, that is, in wealthy industrialized regions, they should be ready to make severe cuts on the carbon emitted. They suggested that the cuts should be at 40% level by the year 2020. Also, the world leaders are called out to at least dispense about $150 billion each year in ensuring that cuts on carbon emission are being made. They explained that they provide an avenue for better adaptation. And this can't be argued since carbon emissions- human impact also play a significant role in the shifting of seasons.

As times expected, it is likely that leaders will just as some non-profitable organization took it upon themselves to fight the problem, government officials will as well be moved to do similar and execute what's needed before we are finally caught up.

Using a particular region to elucidate further the impact of climate change on the season is reasonable and reliable. But do we have one that can stand in for several areas? Yes! A closer example that shows how climate change is impacting the season is what is happening in New Hampshire. This region has been studied, and the result has substantiated further observation that climate change is capable of impacting seasons. In the next subheading, I will be revealing what recent studies and reports disclose and what we can agree with.

### Latest Research on the Impact of Climate Change on New Hampshire

Climate change is having an apparent effect on the season in New Hampshire as revealed by some researchers in Dartmouth and some other colleagues. The warming which is as a result of climate change has impacted different locations around the world. Especially, when there are dramatic impacts on the Arctic and other regions that are vulnerable to an increase in the sea level. Since the implications vary from locations to locations, the effect in the part of England isn't harsh when compared with other areas.

Nevertheless, this study has brought New Hampshire into the limelight. The study reveals that winters have been coming to its end more sooner than expected and the transition period that exists between winter and spring have not been the way it used to be in the past, it has been seen to be longer. It is being recognized that the transition period is opening sooner as each day's temperature rises above the freezing level.

On the report and data gotten, it is possible to project that the interval will have an increase as warmer and relatively less snowy winters is being seen. One researcher even notes further that the longer the transition period, then the higher the impact on the ecosystem. That is, a more extended transition period will implicate the ecosystem. That is why you notice an earlier flowering of plants, the alteration in the timing of the arrival of insects like ticks, black flies, several migrations of birds and animal.

The study indicates that snowpack disappearance happens concurrently with rapid warming of the soil. As a result, when snow covers the ground, sunlight, in turn, jumped off and wouldn't be able to warm the earth below. Then this will make the snow reflect earlier. As it does that, it shows the darker dirt or other types of grasses beneath that, this does more than existing but to absorbs the penetration of the radiation.

What happens as a result of this? It will lead to more heating up, speeding up the melting of the snow and occurrence of mud seasons. Further data proved that the season for natural snow on the ground is ending so fast. And thus, the loss leads to the impact on soil and the corresponding ecosystem. As asserted by another co-researcher, he said: snow is a vital aspect of the plant system, and the loss of this incredible part will mean the loss of the state of soil and the ecosystem in New Hampshire.

Additionally, this impact from earlier melting of the snow had impacted the quick closure of some recreational activities like the fun gotten from hiking. It is highly not a safe adventure to want to try hiking on mud, but if the snow melts so earlier, then what will be made available is mud, which is not advisable to use.

Moreover, the timing and length of the maple sugaring can be drastically impacted. It can also lead to roads becoming harder for driving. Not that alone, it can hinder logging operations. And this is going to affect the business sector as well.

Across the state, something also worthy of note is happening. Take, for example, the data gotten revealed that snow is disappearing sooner, however, the timing of when the trees start to sprout leaves which brings about the end of the transition has often been constant.

It was said that even if the winter is warmer it wouldn't still influence the amount of sun it will have; it is also said that it won't have more than what happened in the previous year. The study covers a more extended period, and it spans over three years. And that jointly represented the range of seasonal climate.

In the first year, it was seen that it was unseasonably warm, fast forward to the third year, it was freezing, and in the second year, it has a moderate cold which is compared to the report three decades ago.

Researcher even included some regions to ensure that the result is gotten from both geographical perspective and timing.

What has been made glaring is that they've been able to predict better what will happen soon, as the temperature tends to be warmer and the snow begins to fall.

Well, frantically, this is agreed to be a starting point and over time if more data are collected, ensuring a more substantial conclusion will be revealed.

As the region has been researched, one of the researchers said that it would be great if such research is made available in other areas too so that this type of conclusion can have a broader range and not just limited to the field of New Hemisphere alone.

These ideas discussed here have validated the claim that climate change is impacting the seasons more adversely. And surely, if the research is being extended to other regions, we can be sure that more claims will be validated.

Now that this chapter has discussed how climate change affects the seasons and accurately, we have checked a region that was recently checked, the New Hemisphere. It is time we consider how we can fight climate change. What may as well be identified as mitigation techniques.

This chapter will cover extensively all the processes involved. It will tell you what you should do to reduce the impact of climate change. Yes, it is evident that the next chapter is your chapter!

**Chapter Eight**

# Climate Change - How You Can Fight it

## Overview

What a long way you've come! From the basics to the least, I've highlighted the impacts of climate change on human existence, water, ocean life, animals, agriculture, the global economy, and the last one, our seasons. You are not a novice anymore to the detrimental impact of climate change. You've seen the data from a scientific perspective, just like I have promised, and while I summed up each chapter, you'd have noticed that each part will have a brief way the menace can be solved. But those economic solutions highlighted would not have gone deeper. What do I mean?

Today, readers are often interested in knowing how they can do things themselves. For example, when advising on how they can come up with some of the solutions on how to combat climate change, even though it is still relevant and enjoyable to tell them to "recharge renewable," it is most appreciated to show readers "how to recharge renewable." Spot the difference? One tells you the mode and the advantage, but the other goes more step further in explaining how anyone willing can do it.

Gladly, this is what I'm dedicated to accomplishing in this chapter. But why did I go this length explaining this? You'd come across some of the ways you can fight climate change, therefore, don't think it is mindless or needless repetition, instead, consider it as a more exhaustive way of teaching you how to go about it; how to bring it closer to your doorstep.

For better capture, ten solid "how to dos" will be discussed in this chapter extensively. Not that alone, I've arranged them in a way that they will be self-explanatory and would capture each region, that is, regardless of where you stay and live, you can apply

175

these great ways of fighting the destructive impact of climate change.

Additionally, I ensured that in each of the ways, at least more than five ways to do it are explained comprehensively. I'm sure to capture what everybody wants, yes, this is what you crave for!

So am I'm just going to fill you to the brim. Happily, if all the previous chapter has gotten you dreaded, this chapter is bent on feeling you will be experiencing brilliant feelings, those of hope and assurance that things will get better if everyone gets busy working toward effecting a better future ahead.

In the aspect of being energy efficient, you might have seen that much have been said on this, but can you do it better, to the point that even the most straightforward behavioral changes will count, and what are these behavioral adjustments? Moving up to the significant changes, what are they? More to it, do you even know what should be the two most important motive for saving energy? You will enjoy seeing the answers.

When it comes to renewable energy, even if as a person who isn't rich, you'd have been searching for ways to get that done, but the question is, how far have you progressed? Nothing yet? It's because you do not know how. Don't even think power plant, think simple pieces of stuff, do you even know that powering up your renewable isn't difficult? Those ways explained will be astounding and will be a great read.

In greening your commute, how many ways do you know? Would you lose count after mentioning taking public transport, carpooling and cycling? The truth is, there is more! More viable means that would feature more technological updates, yes, they are updated methods. Most individuals would not thrash off the idea of putting the price on pollution, but what are the realistic ways to do it? Yes, ten substantial ways will be exhaustively discussed too.

Often time you hear of fuel fossils. How can you excellently divest from this? But many could think that this is meant for big firms and organization. But could that be true, and if it's not true, how can you do it? And the more individuals grasp this aspect, yes, we can eliminate fossil fuels.

Maintaining a stable plant is a sure way to make up for food security. This is a way to tackle global hunger. Sadly, not everyone is equipped on how to go about it, even though small it might be. Also, though food security still holds to be a complex topic, it can be solved. More than five good ways of doing things will have my mention, and definitely, most of the stuff you rarely pay attention will be discussed. In addition to eating in a way to curbing food scarcity, planting trees too will go the greater length to help restrict warming in the environment. But is there any specialty? Are there ways to better do it? And remember that doing it will mitigate the effect of climate change.

Finally, in this chapter, everybody must be on deck working tirelessly so that positive outputs can be reached. But how could that be done without being pushing or demanding? Yes, there are subtle yet effective ways of doing it in the right direction. More methods of teaching that in peoples' heart will be explained.

This chapter indeed is your chapter! Yes, to set it rolling, let's talk about how you can be energy efficient and sustainable.

### Embrace the Attitude of Being Energy-Efficient and Sustainable

Before I begin to mention the ten most likely ways to be energy efficient, let me briefly say the two most prominent reasons why you should often embrace this lifestyle with passion. One is for your benefit, that is, to save your bills on utility, another, is bent on saving others, protecting the environment. Does any of your actions not worth it? Absolutely!

I advise that you stick to every way here, but I already know that you'd like some that you'd want to put them on your scale of preference, however it is be dedicated to sticking to these steps.

1. **Modify Your Day-Day Behavior**. When you tell some folks to be energy efficient, what comes to their mind is going out to the electrical shop and purchase all the energy efficient products out there. Even though this idea isn't a bad idea, yet, that isn't necessarily the only way out. You can begin to be energy efficient by starting with a more straightforward task first. For example, simple stuff like turning off your appliance when leaving for bed or when leaving home is golden. Also, shifting from using high voltage appliances in carrying out your task could be useful, wash manually rather than using a washing machine, dry manually rather than applying a machine dryer.

More to the point is ensuring that you turn off the heat of your thermostat during the winter period, and then making sure that you limit how you use this same facility during summer. This is a significant saving for you! For more efficiency in your home, invest in a home energy monitor that all it does is to keep track of your home electricity usage. It helps you see where the energy you use in your house are going and what appliance is using up your electricity day in day out.

2. **Substitute Your Light Bulbs.** If you use any of the traditional incandescent light bulbs, then be sure to know that these types of light are bent on consuming your electricity usage, mainly. And to keep track of your energy use, you need to seek an alternative. For example, make your purchase on Halogen incandescent bulbs, light-emitting diode bulbs (LEDs) and other compact fluorescent lights consume lesser. They save from 20% down to more than 75% of electricity. A bonus to it is even that they have a longer life span, in fact, 25 times longer!

But know this, the cost of purchase of an energy efficient bulb is highly costly, yet their longevity and energy efficiency make for a better alternative as against the cheaper ones. No lamp could be more environmentally and cost-effective than these energy efficient bulbs discussed.

3. **Adopt Smart Power Strips**. Do you know that even when energy is placed on standby mode, they waste energy? There are some electronics that even when they are turned off, they still consume energy. Astoundingly, it is yet calculated that 75% of the energy that is needed in powering up any electronic gadgets are used up when the power is down. And on a per year scale, it will cost up to $200 per year.

But purchasing this smart power strips will do away with this problem. For better you should set it on off mode at your actual personal time when they haven't been in use. With the help of remote control, you can solve this problem. And if a master device is sent alongside the product, there you go!

4. Install Smart Thermostat. Most times, the stress of turning on and turn off your cooling and heating system might make you want to give up. No! That will be a bad move. Do you know what you can do? Just install the smart thermostat. This will automatically help in eliminating waste. It will turn off automatically when not in use and turns on when there is a need. Thereby, you can reduce the waste of energy. From HVAC systems.

It has been speculated that yearly, your automatic thermostat will save up to $180. There are different types of these programmable thermostats. Some models are for incorporation into your weekly schedule, for some, their concern is on indicating when your system is due for replacement of your air filter or if there is a problem with your entire system. With this, the efficiency of your system can be guaranteed.

5. Buy Energy Efficient Appliances. Now is the time to do that which you've been thinking about. If by schedule, based on calculations, 13% of everyone's total household usage, appliances take up the more significant parts. But how can you do it? Let me open your eyes.

Pay attention to these two numbers, the first price of purchase and the cost demanded running it, annually. Frankly, energy efficient appliance will have a higher price tag and running them will cost around 9-25% other than the other traditional types.

The more important thing to consider is that when purchasing, pay attention to appliances that have on them- ENERGY STAR. The guarantee comes from the federal level. It ensures that less power will be used although the percentage of energy saving level on appliances vary from one device to another. For instance, some energy star dishwashers will require less energy and water, 25% and 45%, respectively. And the refrigerator will cost less power, say 9%.

6.**Limit Water Heating Expenses.** When you need to see one of the culprits; a silent culprit of energy consumption, water heating is to be blamed. It is reasonable to purchase a water heater that is energy efficient, yet it is good to embrace effective ways of using less water heating. So, use less water, turn down or off your thermostat on your water heater. Also, when installing your water heater, insulate your water pipes, both cold and hot. Therefore, when purchasing or replacing your water heater, be sure that you are buying one that is going to meet your actual need and the type of fuel needed to power it.

7. **Just Insulate Your Home.** when it comes to reducing your utility via retaining heat when it's winter time or sending heat off when its summer time, insulate your home! But which area needs to be wrapped? Your basement, attic, floors, and crawlspace are the leading ways that must be protected.

To do these accurately, check the law governing your region first, also pay attention to the verification of your home recommendation because the level of installation is mostly found online. So, just put all these into consideration and let them work for your good.

8. **Make an Effort to Upgrade Your HVAC System.** If you have been using an HVAC system, you'll notice that it has these three: Heating, ventilation, and air conditioning instrument. In regions where they are prone to much cold, especially northern regions, they use more than 40% home energy consumption.

At that rate of consumption, an upgrade will save you a great deal. For example, an update to a U.S. South Energy Star certification will help in saving nothing less than 12% energy on a heating bill which will focus on an approximate per year, $36. Additionally, they are more efficient.

To upgrade, you must at least try and update the ventilation system which is the third component of an HVAC system. Doing that will also improve your energy efficiency. And your ventilation can reduce your heating and cooling cost of running.

9. **Upgrade to Energy Efficient Window.** If you have a window that's not energy efficient, now is the time to get that done. Why? It's only because windows could be responsible for 5-20% of your overall heating bill. Using an energy efficient window will surprisingly prevent heat loss, thus reducing your expenses on heating components. Therefore, buy an energy saving window. Be sure that they come with shades, screen, shutters and other important insulation designs that will help you in preventing heat loss and save efficiently.

10. **Seal Air Leaks in Your Home.** Having buying and installing all the energy efficient appliances, make a double check to confirm if there is no leaking of heat and cold that is going on, because if there are, you will still end up spending more despite switching to energy efficient electrical appliances. Vent, doors, and windows are the three most usual places that offer leakage; check them very well.

While you await the arrival of the technician, you should confirm it yourself. Go near them, notice any cracks or strain. When the technician comes, allow him to run a check too. If you see any cracks or opening, add weather striplings and apply caulk. They are cheap and simple to use.

There you go! The ten practical ways to be energy efficient. But don't forget, mastering a fine behavioral adjustment is the roadway to having all these steps successfully executed. Since every day, technology moves up or scales up, be on the lookout for new technological designs that assure you energy efficiency, either bulb or other electrical appliances. The less heat you consume, the less the power needed to generate it, and that will make up for the demand that's outweighing the supply.

Charging up with renewable is another step to fight climate change; the way to go about it is beautifully carved below.

### Charge Up with Renewables

If you are always on the lookout for how to massively save money on your monthly bills. Do you know you have a close call at your end? Focusing attention on using renewable is the way out.

When you use renewable, you are set for a significant change; you will spend either less or nothing on utility bills. Yes, there is no lie! Just watch it! Let's check into seven of these ways.

1. Install Rooftops Solar Panels. This renewable power source is commonly found around if you are observant. But do you have one? How it works is that the solar panel goes on your rooftops - one of the most efficient ways.  Yes, an alternative, mount them in your yards; not as useful as on your roofs. You'll get to see why!

But, before that how many panels would you need to power your house? Every house based on average usage of energy wouldn't consume more than 1kilowatt of power.

Therefore, based on your latitude and how the panels are being oriented, per square foot, 8-10 watts could be generated. Now back to why I said mounting your boards on the rooftops would be the best options.

If you have a roof that has last a long time, or probably you want a shield off the scorching heat of the sun, installing the panels on the rooftops is the best. You will have to buy solar shingles. You will have standard and recommended rooftops solar panels on your roof. In effect, the solar panels will work for your roof tiles.

So, when the sun is up, enjoy! And when it's down, you'll still enjoy it only if you are ready to part with a few dollars paying for either grid electricity or renewable source of energy.

2. Wind Turbines. Ever seen a wind turbine before? Perhaps you've not been to a wind farm or a floating offshore. Majorly, the wind turbine is so useful for folks with real estates. But if you have a small house, you can still install it? Yes, but it's most advisable for people with several units of apartments.

Even though wind turbines conserve energy, it has a few disadvantages. Noise, ample space, government, and it is not beautiful. Yes, many folks who prioritize on the serene environment and aesthetic, wouldn't want to stay near it.

But some can still insist that since it is a great asset and, in the area, where they stay there is no government placing plan on its use, they will use it. Maybe one of the reasons users are glued to this lower supply is because they are more efficient than solar power.

3. Purchase Solar Oven. Do you bake often? Or probably you make a living from consistent use of the oven. Be ready for a significant change if you want to pick up full use of renewable energy. Most times your daily power consumption may exclude the use of big gadgets. As a result, it is better to create a space for them separately.

Solar ovens are remarkable ways of saving energy. Oven consumes a lot of energy. Yes, a lot! There is a lot of solar ovens sold in the market that you can buy one and start using the sun to process your food. However, if you don't feel like doing that, you might have to meet a builder to build one for you.

The advantages surrounding the use of solar ovens are much. Heating and cooking your food with solar ovens is a one-expense, after paying for the build or the buy, enjoy heating your meal for free. Plus the fact that even during an emergency or power outage, you will still enjoy your meal. You know what that means!

4.Hydropower. On this one, there would be some exceptions. Why? You need water. But if you have your property at a location where there is water, then that's your fortune! What you need to do is divert the stream or river and let it flow via a turbine, and there you go! You have power in your house.

For a fact, setting up a hydropower generator isn't an easy thing! You might need the service of a professional to get it done, though, however, if you have some engineering understanding, yes, building it from scratch is possible.

The advantages of using hydropower are highly abundant. Just like other types of renewable energy, hydropower is stable, efficient and continuous. So, no need to be anxious; you will always get what you should get every time, every day. So, get it straight, and you will reap the bountiful harvest.

5. Install a Solar Water Heater. We all use water every day. Your consumption is subject to where you reside. If you reside in a region where there could be intense cold, this facility is indeed; a must for your home. Solar power isn't just made to function like an electricity generator, as an addition, it can.

When you have water that's been reserved for heating, don't use electricity, the solar water heater will use sun in pumping it through your faucet or any other means. Although gas is cheap, this is cheaper than gasoline or even electricity.

Also, it has a better advantage than using such old panels for the job. This could also make a good alternative when you don't fancy the idea of powering the whole apartment with renewable energy.

When going out in the market, there are several types of them, but before you buy, make a little bit of research, research about the Company's name, year of operation, if nothing you see suggests a long time of service, and no other potential claim or those who have bought can say good thing about it, don't proceed.

Besides being sure that you are investing in quality, be sure of the one that you purchase will serve you the best and right way.

. Solar Air Conditioning. How absurd does it sound to use heat in cooling a home? Most people would want to think: "how does that even connect?" But I tell you, what you have up there isn't a spelling error or a mindless point.

Solar air conditioning uses the heat from the sun to cool your home. To get a closer understanding. Solar panel adopts the mechanics in the water heater. So, among all that gulps up electricity bills in the house, your air conditioning rakes a large part too. And you know more electricity use, more bills. And even you should be ready to spend more if you reside in a hot climate. And surprisingly, you can have more bonus, since the water generated from air conditioning can also be applied for other things. Isn't that remarkable? Sure, it is!

7. Biomass. Its plants waste turn! Amazed? No! I know your concern, pungent smell, and um-kept environment? The use of this alternative energy is so far from that.

This alternate energy uses plant waste. Remember, in your elementary school days, or probably you'd have heard that plants house sunlight and they grow. As a result, you can generate so much hot gas from their waste. And in turn, it can be used for lightning up your light.

Use this alternative if you don't have much on hand and if you have more plants around you. It would amaze you how much you will save.

Fact is, renewable energy is one of the ways we can stop the impact of climate change as the environment warms increasingly. Therefore, keeping the world green is no doubt a marvelous way to achieve the feat. Be reminded that you will save yourself lots of money and that's not all; you will be of help to the community and the world at large.

Also, some parts of the world are suffering from the epileptic power supply. There are so many reasons why this is happening. It could be as a result of damages to the power supply as a result of climate change and improper management, whatever the case may be, relying on renewable energy saves you from this stress and disappointment.

But, why is it urgent that you pick up the use of renewable energy now. It's regrettable that presently, only 5% of the country's energy use is derived from the use of renewable energy, and what is happening to the other 95%, obviously, it's the reliance on non-renewable energy. Undeniably, we have many lengths to travel.

As explored, the common types of renewable energy have been discussed, not that alone, I've shown how each of the renewable energy could be used. Pick one, start the use, it's no hard an idea to start with the one that's is cost-effective for you, where you have the materials to be needed effective. Why not start using today. It might be a pleasant way startup. And surprisingly, in the next 5years, we'd have an extensive record of renewable energy use.

Conclusively, irrespective of who we are and where we live, we all respect a safe environment for ourselves and others. Why not make this a motivating factor to create a more loving environment for the world to live in.

### Green Your Commute

How would you feel if someone tells you to green your commute? Your feelings will reflect your inner person, level of exposure, and what you stand for!

Education plays a vital role in how you make moves that benefit the member of the public. And you see. Greening one's commute is an excellent way to reveal that we are ready to live life at its best - love for oneself and others.

The rate at which folks discharge carbon into the atmosphere is quite alarming that it requires all hands-on deck to get things working in the best possible way. In Canada, for instance, each Canadian spends approximately 26minutes in traveling to work. And when the statistics are further revealed, this was what we've got.

The most significant part, approximately 80% uses car, the closer figure, about 12% commute by public transport, 5.5% adopts walking or trekking while the smallest fraction, 3% uses the bicycles or other forms of transportation. You already know this will have an impact on the quality of air, and traffic congestion.

When you green your commute, you are creating a way of impacting your environment, positively. Even though some of this has been briefed earlier, highlighting them further will be more extensive. Let's learn also.

2. Use More of Public Transport. Commuting via one's private car guarantees comfort, but behind it lies a deadly blow - carbon emission. To work things out well, use mass transit as an alternative to driving daily. If you can do that, at a minimum, you will be saving $800 a year. Isn't that great? But that is not where we are headed.

Data gotten from clean air commute makes it obvious how reliable it is to choose public transport. For instance, they said, a wholly loaded bus would be an alternative for more than 50 cars plying the road, not that alone, a subway would also cater for more than 1000 vehicles on the road. Now you get the drill. There wouldn't be a doubt about cleaner air and less congestion. Considering the cost, there is more to save, as reveal in the same region. In Canada the average price of traveling per person per kilometer is $0.38 higher than the cost of public transport.

The reduction in carbon footprint is immense too, at least a 10% reduction is guaranteed. An excellent save, not so? Do you even have an excuse? Absolutely no! Because in many cities and town, there are several alternative transport systems. There are subways, buses, and trains that have a large capacity of passengers. Thus, choosing this option will be an accomplishment.

It is true that the primary goal here is to reduce carbon emission, but if that doesn't appeal to you. Then, think about five essential benefits you'll reap from the use of this model.

3. Yes, you can get your emails before you toss your leg in your office; you aren't on the wheel, you are an opportunist passenger.

4. With a busy schedule, you have no time to spend on your social feeds. This is your time! Read that book you've wanted to read, listen to music and check on your social feeds.

5. Have access to current news. Even though there are other ways of getting this done, you can still benefit more by reading your local newspaper. What a great thing to do in your comfort.

6. Are you a game freak? Have fun enjoying the pleasure of playing your favorite game. Either a puzzling game that gets you racking your Brian or a racing game that fills you with adrenalin -getting you prepared for the day's work doesn't get better with this.

7. You Can Take a Short Nap. But be careful here not to sleep off past your bus stop. A little idea, if the distance from your place to work will take up to 20 minutes, you can set the alarm for 15minutes, so you can enjoy a 15 minutes relaxation in preparation for the days' work or probably when returning from work.

But here are a few tips to note. Always leave home early if you want to use a mode of public transport, it saves you time and stress. And then you get to work earlier -one of the traits employers are often fond of.

2. Walk, Bike or Run. I categorized these three into one single section because I feel that they are aiming at one goal -moving your body! Exercising makes your body feels so good. It's the best way to have your various body organs to function excellently.

So, choose any of the options either once a week or twice a month. There could be another bone of contention though, that is sweating. But there's a way out.

You can keep your gyms wear on, and neatly arrange your wears in a bag, on getting to work, take a shower, move to the dressing room and dress up! That's been efficient too.

So, if you choose to use the pedal, prepare your helmet and put on your bike shorts. Biking is carbon-free, cheap and fast, did I say that? Yes! For an average person, biking 3.5 kilometers will take him not more than 15 minutes.

Plan and plan. Technology, like we pointed out, has made some preparations so pretty easy. Take for instance, if you choose to walk, judiciously use the navigation application on your phone to make the planning effective. Top of it, you can use Ride to the city to guide tour cycling for mastering routes around your area.

Finally, be safety conscious. If you aren't really on the know about the rules guiding cyclists, read up the lane to use, traffic signs to abide by, your rights on the road and lots more. For pedestrians there are several guides for them too, master these guides. Then, your safety can be guaranteed!

3. Carpooling. If you picked up the reading from the first chapter down here, you can't deny that you have no idea about carpooling. But there's more data I got that made me want to reinforce this point and broaden it a reasonable length.

According to carpooling.ca, it was disclosed that more than 30 million empty seats go to work each day. You see that another way to lessen this waste is to join the carpooling. You can commute along your friends, coworkers and family members.

When you do this, you have up the scale to having the planet saved and would have more money. How would you start? You can by using rideshare program. This will make it viable for you to find a carpool match. Examples of such app are Smart Commute, where you get in touch with other commuters that are heading your way.

So, no hassle in searching, no dull moment if you can even find a karaoke match. That way, you can turn each moment a fantastic one.

4. Ditch the car. Oh Oh! Your luxury? Yes. But remember that's not all you've got. Well as a last resort, it might be an excellent action to take if you specifically stay in the cities where a lot of driving isn't being done. The annual cost of running a car is even more substantial than $10,000, and that figure isn't surprising enough; each car produces nothing less than four tons of carbon emission each year. Now that's troubling.

Even if you have more than one, then this idea should be reasonable for acceptance. It would not reduce your earning. Instead, it makes you save more, and you become more efficient.

If you think you will be robbed of being a car rider, that's a lie. Car sharing offers you a better alternative of making the green life possible. It is also interesting to note that Auto share says their members limit their carbon emission by 1.2 tons every year.

Amazingly, some have even shifted to electric scooters, why not join these if you can't turn to ditch your cars.

5. Scale up Your Specification in a Car. Most times, our specifications might not match up what will be of immense benefit

to the environment. Therefore, we can make some adjustment if we care about ourselves and life. I'm convinced you are.

So, if you wouldn't find the idea of ditching pleasant, then, this at least should make some sense to you.

Make an upgrade to an electric vehicle; that way you can reduce carbon emission. There are numerous regions where you can make an inquiry on the type that fits your need.

6. Buy cars with fuel efficiency., A times you might not just have to give off classic for elegance. Most vehicles that are elegant are very efficient. And those that seem more classic might not be efficient. To get them, check the car out on your country's fuel consumption guide. There you will see estimates for particular vehicles.

Always maintain your car. Always ensure that your tires are well inflated, and regularly keep checking your engine.

7. Telecommute. And yet, this is another incredible solution; if it is being taken up by most people living today, they will end up staying off traffic. At least, if more than a million telecommuters perform their work at home, they will save 250 Million kg of $CO_2$ emissions. If that impresses you, wait for another thriller. Also, if that figure keeps on working further, they can say more than 100 million liters of fuel. We are indebted to technology though because it has made it possible for us to connect with workmates remotely.

How rewarding it will be if everyone can embrace the style. It's a piece of great news that many already have adopted. Join the community and green your commute like a king.

### Put a Price on Pollution

One thing to always have at the back of your mind is that most of the steps to take in cutting your carbon emission or reducing the impact of climate change are interwoven. This will be more evident in this subtopic. Because putting a price on pollution will mean diminishing how much carbon we emit. Either from burning, industrial actions or other negative ways of spoiling the environment.

There are so many ways of reducing air pollution, even a non-specialist would also be able to make mention, but there are some that rarely get our attention, and they should be considered at a grander scale.

Much of the air we breathe in daily are toxic for both animals and humans. So, this isn't a matter of who am I or where I reside. It's everyone's duty! I have ten practical ways of doing it down here. Let me begin with the ones you may not have taken note of.

1. Use Recycled Products. See, if you haven't been doing this, start it now. At least from your next purchase, start by buying only recyclable products. For example, users can use recycled plastics in varieties of ways. It can be used for food packaging, like construction projects, landscaping, street pieces of equipment and other others. For glasses, they can be reused for several numbers of times. It could be used for container manufacturing, for insulation, for brick manufacturing, water filtration, concrete and cement, and many other materials.

These two are the most used products in our day-day activities. Therefore, you can also do further research on how users can recycle other products.

However, recycling reduces the cost of materials, and to the environment, there is little waste that will be sent to the land, thus leading to the havoc on human, plant, and animals. This is a great way to reduce pollution from industries in reproducing new objects, and even if they have to replicate, it will reduce the number and the amount that will be spent.

2. Do Away with Plastic Bags. If this idea isn't helpful to you, then let me spell it out. Plastic bags are tough to decompose. And if

you don't know, there are several alternatives to plastic bags. Hence you need not depend on it. There are leakproof reusable storage bag, reusable produce bag, organic cotton grocery bag, linen bread bag, muslin produce bags, and canvas market bags. Yes, these are alternatives that are essential for you to be remembered, you can search online to see one among the ones I mentioned and see how lovely they are, plus the fact that they are friendly to the environment -because they are reusable!

3. Smoking isn't ideal. You would see that I never asked you to stop smoking. I feel it's insulting. I reasoned: "what if you don't." I've made my judgment. Therefore, if you aren't smoking, that is excellent! But if you do, it's an excellent move to halt it. Smoking isn't just only hazardous to your health but also the health of people. No sane person would derive joy in causing the death of others.

4. Just be Green. Staying on top of the roof in ensuring that you are always on the lookout for how to be environmentally friendly is excellent. A lifestyle that revolves around this does not only gives enough protection to the environment but goes steps further by sustaining natural resources.

5. Educate Others. What would you do if you realize that only a few people are aware of the sad consequences of polluting the air mindlessly? Be smart enough to educate them, help them see the advantages that come from adopting the clean air initiatives, and from the different ways you've learned about, why not tell them?

It is true that you might not get paid in doing this, however, whatever you've done to put people in the know does worth it, you are getting paid by their adherence to whatever they learn. Just ensure you educate in a friendly and intelligent manner, a manner motivating enough to strive to work.

6.Others. Several other ways have been mentioned here. Examples like using public transport, investing in only energy efficient vehicles, planting a garden (much of which will be discussed later), keeping your lights off when you are not home, and make sure you embrace the use of solar power. Doing all these reduce carbon footprint.

Summarily, we should all be sensitive to this issue because, daily, the mortality rate because of air pollution is alarming. If it were to be something, we couldn't find solutions to, then we'd have crossed our arms and watch as it goes on claiming lives. But the reverse is the case. Therefore, it is a must we keep up working actively to reducing our carbon footprint. It's the fight we must win, and we will win.

### Divest from Fossil Fuels

Let's say some years ago someone picks up a prediction that in the coming year, say within the next five year, which this year, 2019, is just three years away from that actual date and said that, there would be an end to the internal combustion time, how would you have reacted. Will you even tell the person that he or she spoke too soon?

Even if you feel that way, then, today's happenings have shown that that prediction is very accurate. It's a great news that divesting from fossil fuel is gradually picking up momentum in the world today. And companies that are closely tied with fossil fuel have seen that many individuals, firms and organizations are backing off. They are withdrawing their funds, stock and investments assets.

Five years ago, many firms and organizations made pledges. Pledges that have been summed into over $50 billion and still progressing. Not denial, divestment is also an incredible way of limiting the impact of climate change on the environment. Well, going through the data, you will realize that mentioning of big companies has only been featured. So many may want to think if an individual can carve a space for themselves in the divestment program.

Well, your reasoning is excellent. Individuals can be in the movement too. So, at every level, all of us can join in the discarding of fossil fuel altogether.

Have not just a sneak-pick, but an in-depth look into the five ways individuals can divest from fossil fuel.

1. Let Renewable Energy Takes All Your Power Consumption. If we are ready for this, we must be willing to make severe cuts, significant changes. Instead of parting a part of your home for non-renewable energy, eliminate it. Ensure that in your house alone, you use renewable energy 100%. Even if it requires more fund, it wouldn't be all day you need to spend money or running, all you need is a few bucks for repair and probably updating the ones you already have. Investing entirely in green energy takes you off fossil fuels. If we can all do that, yes, we will win the war.

2. Stop Buying Petroleum. Although this could be expensive, as time moves on, the price of setting up is set to drop, drastically. Today, you'd find people that have gone electric. That is, it is either an electric scooter, an electric car and yes, they've waved the purchase of petroleum bye-bye.

So, if you can sell off your gasoline car so as to make up for the electric vehicle, if you want to confirm from folks before you head on for the change, it might be unusual to note that they'd all relate how free they've been at least since they aren't faced with the problem of using the gas station anymore. Aren't you ready for this liberation?

3. Live Locally, Limit International Traveling. Indeed, some might even suggest total cutting off of flights. But I won't advise that emergencies may arise and some other time, unforeseen event. You might want to make some critical journey. Thus, one of the advisable things to do is to limit unnecessary journeys. Cut them down to the barest minimum. Limiting your traveling is saving the world from the most important consumption of fossil fuels.

4. Divest all Your Investments from Fossil Fuel. Some organizations you partner with likely support that which you stand for. Move off and seek for those that support what you stand for.

5. Teach Others. If you are an employer of labor and you so much crave for divestment from fossil fuel, you have to let your employees divest from your fossil fuel from all of their assets.

**Eat to Maintain Stable Planet**

Do you know that what's good for the earth is good for the body? This isn't from me, but I agree with it. But whose footprint is this? Is the group of dietitians across the globe. They are increasing their concern on the environment, and yes, they agree to that statement: "what is good for the earth is good for the body."

To limit the consequences climate change brings on the environment, significant changes need to be made in what we eat. That is, we have to eat and cause a balance and not imbalance.

Here below are the recommended steps to take if you'd want to make the earth stable and put a stop on the rapid change.

1. Eat More Beans. Yes! If you're a regular fan of this meal, it's time to up your rate, ear more! How about you not a fan at all, it's time for refining unless if you have allergy or intolerance. If none of these affect you, ride on. But why must you ride on?

Beans are densely packed with protein, Folic acid, and fiber. Yes, seeds are around everywhere. And more bonus, it has low fat. And more importantly, it has just a small fraction of carbon footprint. So, try it now and enjoy seeing your skin glow.

2. Feed More on Sardines. Sardines are small fish. But they are sustainable and is packed with Vitamin D and Omega-3 fatty acid. Even if you aren't a fan, you can stick it in another vegetable to get the best of the meal.

For instance, tomatoes would form a better pair with fantastic seafood. Yes, sustainability is the goal. With sardine, you are on track.

3. A little Shift to Organic Meal and Vegetables. Flee from any favorite chemically grown vegetables and fruits. The primary reason is that most of the fruit is covered up with pesticides residues - chemicals that are harmful to human's health. They are believed to cause cancer in living human. Then, if you require vegetables, be sure to get them from environmentally friendly farmers or group that are rated by most buyers.

4. Stay Glue with Protein-Based Vegetables, Fruits, Nuts, and Seeds. If we can improve how much protein we get from the plant, say a 10% increase, it will be benefiting our health, and it will benefit our plants. Though incorporating them might seem hard, you might not be sure which one are you to go with. Here are a few options for your pick. If you can use all, high, options like peanuts, lentils, quinoa, and chia seeds are sustainable and would make you a great deal.

5. Pasture-Based Egg is an Excellent choice. Of course, you'd expect pasture-raised eggs to be of vital importance than any other eggs from another source. And you have a point. Pasture-raised eggs have abundant omega-3 Fatty acid and more and more Vitamin D.

Positively, they have great flavor, sufficient protein to keep you satisfied throughout the morning. Lastly, eggs are known to be climate-friendly means of animal protein. Eating eggs, it doesn't get safer and better!

6. Consume Low Quantity of Pasture-Fed Beef and Dairy. More research has shown more valuable noteworthy points. First, between the two types of feeds for animals - grass fed beef and grain fed beef, grass fed beef stands more preferred. Why? It has more antioxidants and less inflammatory fatty acid, all of which are absent in a grain-fed animal.

Take, for instance, milk gotten from a grass-fed cow will produce Omega 3 fat that will guarantee a reduction of inflammation. And it has the potential of reducing the risk of Type 2 diabetes and other heart diseases. And when grain is even used in feeding rather than grass, the environmental impact becomes higher, as against the use of weed.

7. Stay Off Highly Processed Food. That snacks you gladly eat with comfort may come with additional chemicals. And that's as a result of the use of some chemicals to make the preservation or the chemicals used in producing the containers used. And if the plastic used for the container is disposable, it added to the battle the land has to wrestle. Because materials like that are hard to decay, they are hardly being recycled. Making a terrible issue for the planet earth.

Sadly, regular consumers are viable to diabetes because of the excess sugar used in the production of these processed foods.

8. Bottled water. Funny huh? No! I'm an advocate of regular intake of water. That is, drink more water every day. But the idea of using bottled water? No! It doesn't seem friendly. Even though most folks who resort into drinking water do so because of the hygiene. It has been verified that bottle water does more harm than the supposed good benefits.

To solve the issue, go around with your water bottle, there, you will keep your water in there for drinking when you feel the urge to drink. I do same, and if at all you go to work with a bag, you will stylishly add the bottle in bag. Or use any of the containers described earlier on as an alternative to take your water to work comfortably. Some are even well designed which will comfortably stay within your hand.

9. Cut on Salmon and Tuna. Fresh fish is an excellent option for eating, but to think of salmon and tuna, no, that's not environmentally friendly. These types of fish are called flesh-flown

fish are they aren't sustainable, even if they are, they are the least durable.

10. Stay Off Any Conventionally Raised Diary or Meal. They are filled with higher carbon and requires more water when compared to their counterparts, pasture-based counterparts.

In addition to those as mentioned earlier. They require lots of antibiotics, and that impacts the surrounding land and water negatively.

Feeding on the pasture-raised diary is better than these. It's certain that poultry owners see that most people are keen about being environmentally friendly; they will be forced to adopt that style nicely.

Also, eating in a way that keeps the food in the globe circulated is an excellent way to a sustainable lifestyle. If everyone does that, we can be confident of food security at any level we crave for. These are some of the ways you can get this done. It's not a wizard plan; preferably it is a plausible plan.

1. Food and Nutritional Security Should be Balanced. Focus has previously been laid on solid foods. I'm sure the idea was all about tackling hunger. But that isn't where all our energies should be diverted into; we need expansion.

We have to go past calories consumption and check into the balance of nutrition. That concern is made on maize; the same interest should extend to all types of crops to ensure that there should be more balance between staple and horticultural crops. That's the roadway to sending malnutrition to the coffin.

Further, farmers should be well informed on how best they can mix crops to get balanced nutrition. So that it wouldn't be less in one and large in the other, it will inevitably result in a significant imbalance shortly. Also, more education is needed for them so that they can have more quality seeds to plant and grow.

2. Use Technology Judiciously. Yes, technology offers a modern way of addressing some petty problems that might later aggravate into a big problem if not quickly checked. Modern IT should be introduced to local farmers. They need to be trained and expertly guided so that they can have the best output and not just improving yield alone but ensuring that they maintain the environmental standard.

3. Equip more young people into the system of agriculture. The number of young men and women who leave towns and villages to cities is growing each day.

They firmly believe that no future is in agriculture. Possibly they are glue to the positive side and the adverse effect of having low produce. Prices of food will go higher, more people to survive, might have to leave the city for the villages where there might still be something to fall back on.

The government should then be ready to help this one pursue a career in agriculture. If they have the passion for it, let them have access to equipment and machine that need to be purchased at subsidizing rate or rather, the government will give them free loans that they will pay in installments.

Alongside the help, they need to be taught the best way to practice their work to maintain an environmentally friendly attitude.

Indeed, there is more to be done. Both from your consumption and that of the government.

**Plant Trees.**

In tackling climate change, more trees define more clean air, the carbon present in the atmosphere is set to be absorbed comfortably and conveniently.

But if you are told to plant trees to contribute your quota in solving climate change, do you have any idea which one you'd plant? Well, if that's your condition, you need not to worry, many too are confused too. One of the reasons why they are confusion is because regions differ from each other. What will work in one area might not even feel the taste of life in another.

Also, Scientists offering "lots" are only contributing to the confusion already existing. But that's not a big issue if scientists themselves can recommend planting lots of trees, doing otherwise wouldn't yield real reward.

If you need to plant lots, you will still have to answer the question of what specific species? Well as an answer to the question, I'd advise you plant a variety of species. Scientists wouldn't start telling you this specie is wrong or this is good.

Even though some organizations might help you in identifying the species you need to plant, but scientists would still advise that you plant varieties. To add to that, I will say don't plant them close to either your wall or fence, unless they are trees with a taproot.

Another reason why it is highly reasonable to invest in diversity is that you never can tell what will happen in the future. For example, pest could come and feed on the native species you have, what happens, some of them would die off destabilizing the purpose they serve. But if for diversity, they affect one and leave the other.

Another thing is that you shouldn't assume too high. Because most of the assumptions regarding tree planting might not work, and this might deter us from planting mew diversity or variety.

We might reason that they would need more special condition or treatment and which in the actual sense might not demand that. They might survive well and better than we think.

Ultimately, plant several trees and many species. That is the only plausible way to solve the problem, yes, the only way to be aware which type will survive and be saved.

So now, let's put it closer, when you need to plant a tree either for your landscape, rather than imitating a neighbor needlessly, first demand the service of a landscaper.

Tell him what you need. A tree with similar qualities with either the one you see around or the one you've seen somewhere. Your landscaper knows better than you. The landscaper understands this better and will provide you with best that will match your need. Although, some of your consideration might include height, color shape, and bark. Aesthetic, elegance and other several factors will influence what choice you will finally go with.

And finally, let's talk about ten random things to always do every day to assist you in fighting the problem of climate change.

1. Resolve to Use Natural Light. Using natural light during the day will save you more, in fact, more than what both renewable and non-renewable energy could proffer. So, where will this energy be most efficient? In your workplace during the day. More designs from architect have started featuring most of the developed world industrial offices need of light.

It gladdens the heart to note that on June 16, this year, many firms will have to create an awareness of using natural light instead of using an electric light bulb, they would turn off their light.

2. Save Water. If you live in a region where water scarcity is hard, or you've read about what future event will bring, and water scarcity is mentioned among them, save rainwater more than ever before and use it efficiently. Since you had little stress getting the water, you might be tempted to use without great care and caution. Therefore, always have this close to you: if you use it wisely, you are extending the days of going through hell to get water. Capping it, there are several articles online that gives more details on how to manage stormwater.

3. Purchase Furniture Made of Sustainable Material. Just because you are in need of wood furniture, you might want to jump into any furniture maker you come across. Even if you have the urge, exercise patience. Only buy sustainable wood that cares about the environment and not one that is mindless of his action.

4. Renovate, Don't Buy. Ask any preservationist around, and you will see that one of the greenest homes is the one that has been built already. But one problem that is usually found with an old house is the consumption of electricity. A solution to that is speeding up the standard to 21st century standard of electricity efficiency. So, scale up, use renewable the more and more.

5. Limit Food Waste. We must strive to solve food waste. You have to plan well before you start any cooking. Other things that need to be check into is how you store your food and how you preserve them. If accurately done, you can have the best approach to peddling down food waste.

6. Plant Your Own Garden. Rather than going the extra mile in checking the source of a vegetable you are going to plant. Get your natural and local garden where you can be sure of the source. And you can be confident that you are eating real local vegetables and not some chemically grown alternative.

7. Stop Your Engine. When stopped to be checked by any road warder, if it's going to be past 10 secs, turn off the engine. It helps you save more fuel and keep the carbon discharge very low and minimal.

8. Listen to Podcast About climate. Keeping yourself updated to the current trend about climate change will help you to know the next alternative plan to take in caring for your community. That way you can keep up with latest and current development. And the earlier information gets to you, the fast you inform others and acts.

9. Read a Book. Has this book not served as an eye-opener for you? It has proven as a guide for your learning about climate

change. There are other books too that would make a great read about climate change. They will assist you in knowing what is going to happen in the world, the current situation and the suggested solution you need.

10. Be an advocate. I know of a man who says rather than assuming they are polluting the world, he said we are polluting the environment. Now ask me what his point is? If you litter your environs, you are also contributing to the drastic change in climate. So, what should you do, if you'd not desire to be among those who are running the earth, it is simple, don't throw litters around. Dispose of waste properly, when you catch sight of someone not doing it the right way, call them to order, teach them!

11. Be More Concern When Advocating. Indeed, when advocating, you might have the urge to sound too rigid. But don't do that. Just be considerate, speak in a friendly and calm manner, let them see the benefit and not the tone of pride and arrogance. Let them see the genuine concern for the environment and not as a task that awaits a reward. How endearing you will become if you adopt it that way.

Finally, we've come to the end of this chapter. You've got the categories, how it could be done, on renewable, being energy efficient, planting a tree, the food you eat, how to green commute, and divesting from fossil fuels. All these are incredible ways of fighting climate change that I've discussed.

This has led to the final part of this book, that is climate change adaptation. How can one adapt in the face of a constant change of adjustment? In the next chapter, we'll answer a few questions like what an adaptation is, what is climate adaptation, what and how you can adapt to climate change, options available and lastly, we will check ten excellent way to adapt to climate change.

**Chapter Nine**

# Climate Change and Adaptation

**Overview**

The preceding chapter has helped us see several ways in which we can successfully fight the drastic change in the climate. And it has cover from the basics down to the whole part. But looked intently, it majors on "reducing carbon print." However, reducing carbon print isn't enough; we have to step up, go further in ensuring that there are other supportive techniques. The world at large is now more than ever before battling with an increase in temperature, seasons shift and more extreme weather events. Thus, adaption is a must for every country.

For examples, today, many nations have started realizing that the reduction of carbon footprint isn't the only goal that should be set before us all. Instead, we must have other preventive techniques. Thus, many have begun adapting to the climate change. To scale it up further, did you know that even the world's policymakers have realized that this step is inevitable? For instance, in the 2015 Paris agreement, included in it, for the very first time in the organization's history set an adaptation Goal. Likewise, two years ago, in 2017, the United Nation Climate conference that was held in Bonn with several officials from various countries marching on the same goal- climate adaptation. It is highly incredible that nations around the world are going more faster and unitedly, they've agreed upon having National Adaptation Plans - NAPs.

Furthermore, the UN climate Change Adaptions Section carved out four key areas; these areas are:

Ecosystem-based Adaptation. In the time of adaption, they've incorporated projects, plans that make judicious use of biodiversity and ecosystem options and services as part of the essential philosophical adaptation strategy.

Access to Adaptation Finance. This aspect includes the assistance and helps given to countries all over the world so that they can have access to finance that will assist them in building resilience and within their capacity. For every state, this is a highly rewarding concept.

World Adaptation Science programme. This includes grants and designed of an interface between the adaptation research community, that is, those that are filled with the responsibility of researching into the modern adaptation techniques and decision-makers, those who verify and confirm if a current adaption technique is going to be welcomed or nullified.

Knowledge, Analysis and Networking. Without adequate networking, there will be a delay in the sharing of information about adaptation from country to country. Therefore, this aspect allows the dissemination of information regarding adaptation knowledge over well- connected global networks.

These four techniques are sure to go a long way in ensuring further highly efficient adaptive methods.

Moreover, the European Union are also intervening in the adaptation techniques, and you could wonder why they should be concerned when most of their countries are serving as hosts for numerous refugees who fled their respective countries for this continent as a result of the havoc wreaked upon them by climate change.

The truth is, at all levels of administration, there is a severe need for adaptation strategies. In the international, national, regional and local level it is highly essential. In Europe for example, the severity of climate change impacts varies from one region to the other. Therefore, most of the adaptation techniques curated will have its execution at the local levels. In addition to that, the strength and ability to adapt has also varied from one population to another, economic aspects and regions across Europe. The inclusion of this strategy is necessarily helpful because the impacts of climate change overshadow the boundaries of individual states. Thus, the intervention will also do well in ensuring continuity of developing adaptive strategies.

Also, some unfortunate regions will be assisted as well. They will have the benefits from the areas advantaged down to their neighborhood. Therefore, they will be able to pick up the needed adaptive techniques for survival.

Also, adaption should not be taken for lightly. Because the faster climate changes, then adaption techniques should be carved out for that. But if otherwise, then, there will be more difficult and as such more money will go into the policy-making, not that alone, meeting up with the damages it has caused will also take a long time.

Therefore, as climate change is rapid, then adaptive techniques should excellently do too. As you proceed, you will get to see that adaption will come in different shapes and forms. Because the way a particular community will design the way they combat the changes in their fight will be different from another region. Also, how successful adaptation techniques will be is not centered on the governments alone; it also includes all major stakeholders in the public and private sectors.

But there is more, from research, we have seen that some plants are adapting to some changes in the environment, others haven't. Checking further, it has been investigated that there are factors responsible for these changes; that is, there are reasons why some plants and animals are not adapting. What are those factors?

To enable you to gain answer into the question, it is essential that we learn about what adaptation is, how it connects to climate change, how some plants have adapted (you will read some examples), what are some adaptation options and lastly, practical ways humans can also adapt perfectly.

At first, let us start examining what adaptation is. And the branches it has, after that, we can move further in understanding varying degree of understanding climate adaption.

**What is Adaptation?**

Simply defined, an adaptation is identified as a genetic change or mutation that aids organism, as an example, plants and animals to survive in its habitat - environment! As a result of the most frequently aiding nature of the mutation techniques, this aspect is transferred from one generation down to the other. And when more and more organisms inherit the mutation, the mutation then tends to become part of the species automatically. In another hand, we would say the variation has become an adaptation.

Moreover, there are some biological definitions of adaption that would also shed light on some critical aspects. For example, it is further explained that adaption is an evolutionary stage of living species either plant or animal to reside in its habitat and it is capable of reproduction - apparently that suggests a favorable condition.

You know that the environment is not permanent, that is it changes - talking about natural change here. So, as it turns, these organisms have to do the same, they have to keep adapting to the changing of the environment. Thus, many run this line as being parallel to evolution (we aren't going into this).

Now, what would you say is the primary reasons why dinosaurs have gone extinct? It is plainly because they could not adapt to the changing environment, and back then, it was even natural climate change and not the one experienced today. Additionally, there are stages of human adaptation many years ago that has brought man into this modern stage. All of this is regarded as an ecological adaptation.

There are numerous examples of adaptations in our lives today. At least, we can expect that when we observe that when we go into the hot sun for a longer time, we experience a tan. And what does that mean? It means how our skin adapts to the heat and Ultra Violet radiation that comes from the sun. And this is how the process works:

When the exposure to the sun increases, the presence of melanocytes in the skin automatically increase the production of melanin. The function of the melanin is the help absorb the heat and thus lead to the protection of the nucleus, and ultimately, it will lead to the safeguarding of the DNA from mutation as a result of the Ultra Violet rays.

In addition to how humans have reacted to the adaptations of the sun, animals too have for a long time proved to be adaptive, they've carried out the process in such a dignified way. For instance, the giraffe that is now identified as the tallest animal species on earth didn't come to be like that from the start. Then what happened? Could it be an adaptation? Let's confirm that.

You see, those years ago, there were intense competition in the bushes among some category of animal, you know giraffe are animals that solely feed on herbs, and thus they can call herbivore. This competition makes survival difficult. Some plants and trees that serve as food for giraffe grow taller; then it is now necessary for the giraffe to get an increase in the neck which now affects the overall height. They have to stretch their necks so that they can have something to feed on; they keep on reaching for taller trees in the bush.

The giraffe isn't the only animal I can get to point out that has the incredible ability of adaptation. Animals that live in severely cold weather have developed an adaptive technique too; they have tiny limbs and ears. To what advantage? They have a smaller surface area which in turn mean the reduction in heat from the body will be a bit less than animals with such design. To add to that, some of these animals possess fur, thick fur and have fat around their body that assist them in the proper level of insulation, which makes the fighting of cold possible and realistic.

In the desert too, animals have adaptive techniques that will allow them to survive even in the most extreme condition, where there exists lack of water, for example, in the desert.

Take, for example, the Camel, known as an animal, that drinks a lot of water. Credits go to the storage tank that camel has, the tank could be found in the humps. Therefore, it might not be surprising how they go days without water when you realize that the bumps will be used by Camel to carry on with their survival by taking from the reserve they have.

Also, toads camouflage, they have an impressive ability to align with the changes in the environment. And this is also an example of adaptation. There is a form of adjustment that excellently serves as a warning- The Monarch Butterfly.

The last category, plants too have excellent adaptation techniques. Plants that are found in the desert all have their strategy for limiting the water loss in their body, so they have something to drink. They have seen survival techniques when compared to the camel. An example of such a plant is the Cactus plant.

Cactus plants in the desert have leaves that have been naturally reduced to look identical to the spine, and their stems have layered or covered with what is known as "waxy coat." The function of this coat is to reduce the loss of water from them.

Going back to human, other adaptive techniques have been developed concerning the ways they adapt to the sun. Scientists have seen that humans develop an increase in Red Blood Cells, and this is a response to adaptation. This is being noticed when they are climbing higher altitude where there is a decrease in oxygen, they develop more red blood cell and breathe heavily.

Adaption isn't only based on physical change alone, and it goes beyond that. It reveals some biological differences as well. When there is a need to avoid extreme cold, some animals will go on hibernation mode, for some bird who can excellently do well with adaptation, they travel away from the colder region if that will even require traveling many miles, to get a warmer climate.

There is one true sense from the non-forced, natural adaption. And that is, nature can balance itself even in extreme cases. It is thus clear that any typical or unique characteristics developed either by animal or plants, which make them survive in a particular environment are identified as the adaptation.

Interestingly, there are different classes of adaptation. They are into three, even though we have been briefed in the earlier aspect of "adaptation." There is a more comprehensive understanding that has to be gained. Else, it won't be possible understanding all the essential and vital aspects of adaptation, and these are needed so you would have excellent skills of adaptation.

1. Tropical Rainforest Adaptation. In any tropical rainforest, the weather condition is usually wet and hot. For a further breakdown, it is estimated that there are more than 80 inches of rain each year. Plants in the tropical rainforest, however, have the kind of adaptation that allows them to shed water effectively. To make the purpose count and work effectively, their leaves are often in drips tips.

In furthering their survival, they have buttress and stilt roots, and these are essential for the trees that are being browned in these areas.

Also, tropical rainforest plants have to take in whatever sunlight is available in the dark forest floor. In this region, comfortably you will find large leaves, and experiment shows that large leaves are capable of absorbing sunlight well. There are several plants like orchid, fern, and bromeliads that have adapted to growing like epiphytes very tall where there is abundant sunlight. Plants in this region naturally adapt well.

Desert Adaptation. A few examples that have been related in the preceding paragraphs can give you a clue on how plants and animals fare in this region. In this region, the weather condition is usually and generally hot and severely dry. And with be type of state, we can come to see how well plants and animals could show their adaptation.

In this region, there is a need to adapt due to lack of water availability. Many plants in this region have expandable stems that are being used in storing water efficiently. For others, their inability to possess storage in their system have designed the techniques that would discourage water loss in their body.

For several animals that stay in the desert, they have many adaptative techniques to ensure a higher survival rate. For example, some animals are nocturnal. This means they have a mood alternation for the use of energy only when the condition is favorable. More to the point, they will act when its chilly night - for proper reservation of energy and nutrients, and then during the hot day time, they either hibernate or become less active - to prevent loss of nutrients and energy. It's surprising that kangaroo would excrete solid urine as against liquid directly because it aims at conserving water.

Other Forms of Adaptation. Did you notice that the two forms of adaptation discussed are an adaptation to specific climate? That is desert climate is a climate on its own, tropical climate is a climate on its own. Thus, we can ask, do we have other types excluding these specific types? Yes!

There are several aspects of the environment that organism adapt favorably to as well. For example, in adapting, some animals would adjust to eating a specific type of food. For others, their adaptation isn't about what they will eat, and it is avoiding the habitat where they could be eaten up by other animals.

For some with behavioral adaptation, when they need a mate for the production of young ones, their pattern of adaptation assists them in having one. Take a view into what happens to this plant. Some plants have developed many structures that have helped them in pollination. And this becomes so due to the insect they attract.

So, in a sense, they wouldn't be denied reproduction. As you can see from tropical to desert, and other types of adaptation, plants, and animals have been excellent examples of adaptation, and they've shown how natural adaptation could bring about balance in the ecosystem

However, one can still wonder, since the climate changes that occur naturally is helping these organisms adapt well in their environment, would their form of adaptation have a replacement since climate change is drastically occurring and it influences how the climate change. Well, this question would lead us to answer and knowing what climate change adaptation is. Yes, it's going to be a full read too.

### What is Climate Change Adaptation?

As indicated earlier on at the overview, the world as one has to fight the emission of carbon into the atmosphere, but adaptation on the other flip is not really sung by the world, while some parts see it as a way of addressing climate change better in collaboration with the reduction of greenhouse carbon emission, others are riding in the comfort of reducing their carbon footprint alone.

This section will discuss all the concept exclusively one needs to know about Climate change adaptation. Generally, from the Adaptation meaning as its being related to Climate change, it is the process whereby an entity prepares well in advance for climate change. But sadly, Adaptation is viewed as the alternative to the fighting of climate change, and mitigation has revealed numerous attentions from the world, in fact picking up from the grass root. As seen in chapter eight, all the steps in reducing carbon footprint are regarded as mitigation. Its central theme is limiting the contribution to the problem of climate change. And that's what you've read about.

Even though while presenting my analysis, I didn't speak of adaptation first, then analyze mitigation second. Instead what I did was to discuss mitigation first and now am I explaining Adaptation. I'm in no way downplaying or peddling down the importance of adaptation to climate change; only, I just made it hold the second phase in my explanation.

And although looking at it in a reasonable and straight form, adaptation and mitigation are also closely linked; the dominant theme is summed as: "helping to cope better with drastic climate change." Either it comes second, or not adaptation is an exciting aspect of climate change, we must all learn about it.

Right though, research about Climate change adaptation is referred to as being a confused field of research, and those in the research process are working tirelessly to develop to make sense from the study so that it wouldn't be an "abandoned project." Well, it doesn't appear to me as a surprise and why did I say that? You'd agree with me that to prepare the whole world, the physical and infrastructure aspects for climate change isn't an easy task, thus confirming its complexity should be anticipated and expected.

It might be that you've gone through some research books that speak strongly about adaptation, and questions like what is adaption, which is even adapting and what do we adapt to? I've prepared this part in a way that from the basics of adaption right to the grass root, you'd rightly say: What's next on adaption. Well, let's briefly understand the adaption cycle. That's a step forward.

### Adaptation Cycle.

For you to understand adaptation in the right way, I'll make it appear to you as a cycle. I believe that to be an excellent way to make you know it better.

Picture yourself as the one in charge of governing a city, and on a day while you are enjoying a delicious meal with your family, you heard it being reported in the news that climate change is set to cause disasters, havoc, and wreck. It will not only affect structures, but it will also impact the economy and health. Now, since you are in charge of governing a city, would you sit and let the event hits the city you are ruling? You will want to get ready and make preparation ahead of the disaster that looms.

But to accomplish that, there are series of steps you will have to take, not so? These steps will be channeled at making your infrastructure and services excellent, and therefore, you will be able to function as designed. These lead us to the actions that you'd want to take:

*1. Identifying the Exact Climate Hazard that is Set to Occur.*

*2. Determining the Risk*

*3. And Select Adaptive Options.*

*4. Implementation*

*5. Monitoring*

Let's pick this step or process one after the other. (Still, put yourself in the picture of the person governing the city)

1. Identifying the Exact Climate Hazard That is Set to Occur in a Region. Now there is an average forecast that might likely be set to occur in a region. Now in your area is your district expected to be wetter, hotter or drier? And as a result of this change, is it going to impact or bring about pest infestation that has never been around? Or probably will this bring about extreme weather events such as thunderstorms, heat waves, and other extreme weather events? Will they happen more frequently or once in a while?

For you to gain the proper answer to the question, it's right to look at global, regional and national verification. For some countries, they have checked into these questions at both national scales, and they've provided reports that have been made open to the public. In addition to what some countries have done, the United Nation present reports every five years through IPCC.

However, there are some specific impacts in precise locations that are extremely hard to make predictions about. And that is one of the challenges of adapting to climate change. Although the models generated by climate change are often presented at continental levels and bringing this data down to smaller areas are expensive. But gladly, many climate scientists are tirelessly working towards improving climate projections thus making it possible for everyone to understand the risk involved.

No country or region can be explicit about the type of climate impact they will have to battle with, regardless, the smaller the scale, the more climate unreliability.

In central North America, they have high confidence as to what will happen in the year 2050 and going into the region, in Winnipeg what climate change they will face is so uncertain even in the year 2024.

What can we sum up here? Continually, global climate models are bringing it down to ensuring accuracy, however, bringing their skill to the local level is still a challenge that must be won. Nevertheless, since at local levels we can be sure of the exact impact the climate change would bring, to an extent you can dwell on the global scale. But since the study isn't halting, we are confident that over time, we will arrive there, and as a result, you can know what hazard might befall you.

Summing it up, once the type of hazard that is going to happen is evident, what you need to know next is the link between your services and the dangers that are coming. Thus, figuring what is likely to occur when the climate change happens is needed to be known, because that is what will lead you the next stage, identifying the risk involved.

Identifying the Risk. Just as being sure about the precise climate hazard that will occur is difficult, risk itself is another broad area in social science. It has even been in existence way before the issue of climate change sets in.

You might think that risk is related to only natural hazards, but that is not true, it goes beyond that, in fact, it extends to both crime, giants, technology, terrorism and several others. Since it has a broader scale, the risk of the theory is generated.

To start with, the definition of risk varies from one individual to another. What you value might be different from me. Thus, we can say that risk is based on what individual value and on that, it might even move up and be political. Some scholars, who study risk as a "subject" have also defined it as a sort of equation, whereby they say that risk is equal to the tendency of hazards times the impacts of that type of hazard hitting any system, be it social or political.

In another definition, it is seen as a function of exposure to havoc and a person's susceptibility or system's vulnerability. In some system, in assessing the risk that is set to occur in a city, some city engineers can say with confidence and precisely what a 1cm inch precipitation in summer could mean to the local sewer; however, it is difficult to discover or have a straightforward calculation in other forms of system.

Let's pick another instance. Let's say we have two trucks on the highway: One is a 4×4 truck designed with winter tires and another KIA Rio that is designed with summer tires. On this highway, they are exposed to one specific type of hazard, heavy snowfall. Let me ask you, will the truck face less risk?

It might just appear to be so but not necessarily the case. Take for instance, the driver in the KIA Rio has a fully charged phone, inside the car with him is a blanket, and the primary motive of setting out on a trip is just to collect a draft from a co-worker who gave him no actual fix time for coming, really, he wouldn't be okay with the inconvenience they encounter, however, they will still be okay. On the other side, the driver in the truck is just putting on a short, and a linen t-shirt, with him, is a small child and no cell phone. Now, in the kind of scenario, which one has the highest risk? You've got a change of mind. Excellent!

That little highlight helps us to see that our attention has shifted from the car now, and has landed on those in the vehicle, and specifically those who face more risk.

And mainly, this has gone further to show us that calculating risk isn't more straightforward nor can it be calculated without values. Therefore, it is vital that governments that are passing through an adaptation process will examine a different type of inputs and thus effect a legal and working way of addressing the issue.

Thus, for proper risk evaluation, the people in authority must be sure of what an acceptable risk is or not. Thus, identifying this will help them in proffering solutions to what and see which preparation would be a waste and which development will be sufficient. If there are more fund, can they make provision for both risks? And they scrutinize it to see which one will be of paramount importance. Whichever one will strike their attention they must prepare ahead.

We can now conclude that once a nation has explicitly seen what the climate impact will be all about and they have identified the several risks involved within their area, there is a need to move to the next stage of execution, which is selective adaptation.

3. Selective Adaptation. This adaptive option solely depends on the effect and the risk identified. That is, the type of wreck the climate change will bring, and the number of risks involved. Take, for instance, if a city is expected to experience more increase in precipitation, they may decide to limit or change project plans from investing into concrete surfaces to surfaces that will allow for proper absorption of water. Thus, they can reduce the impact of flooding.

However, there might be some individual that would frown at that idea, so in a bit to meet up or provide an alternative, they will have to purchase a sewer system that has more capacity for severe rainfall.

Several adaptive tasks can be carried out for each unique specific climate hazard. Governments of the land might have to increase how people get the message across the globe or informing them on how it will likely affect their behavior. Also, it could also mean the developing industrial building or erecting of structures that will cater for the occurrence.

In selecting, there are several things they have to consider. Some of them include and depend solely on the type of technology available to the member of the public, and then the resources (finance, human resources), it also includes the ideology, how accepted and the willingness to execute the idea.

Even though there is a selection of adaptation actions, there are several questions that need to be asked for proper implementation. Some adaptive techniques that are designed out will be glaring to them, but others might not be to the government which will approve the application. At least larger stormwater sewers might be constructed to cater for the excess rainwater. On the flip side, other adaptation strategies might not be visible and will be channeled in a various number of ways.

Recall that I mention the idea of limiting the number of impermeable surfaces to reduce flooding. The idea has been at loggerheads with the law of the country of a land. So, implementing that might not be practical. If they apply that, it might mean that government will set up a new law that will allow builder to invest in green roofs or probably reducing the number of surfaces that will not allow the percolation of water in the ground thus reducing flooding.

What is so important here is that those who are in care of adaptive measures should ensure they convince those in power on how the crucial the implementation is needed. And what will likely happen, the economic impact if nothing is done, although at every stage they have to be objective and critical about every step, this is to show that it will end up a good process in the long run.

However, once they've agreed on the type of implementation techniques they will need, and the adaptation could come in differing forms, then implementation comes to reality. And that takes us to the next stage.

**Implementation.**

I have to remind you that every stage of the adaptation process or cycle is crucial. And before any alteration is made, careful planning, observation must be in place and effect what should happen at this stage.

Before deciding on implementing it, they have to be sure and once approved, it must not be delayed or slowed down. All steps leading to successful implementation must be checked, unless if there are circumstances that are beyond human control that set in if not, it must be carried out as planned.

Therefore, all individuals involved must have the goal in sight, to activate all resources assigned to the implementation and successfully deliver the action plan. Well, unity and working as a team are intrinsically valuable, on that note success would be guaranteed.

Also, in implementation, the relevant tools must be used. If appropriate tools are judiciously applied, it can impact the success of the ultimate result that will be gotten. However, if not ask, there would be problems, and that will hinder progress.

While the execution, monitoring should be incorporated. The monitoring team has an enormous task resting on their shoulder as well.

5. Monitoring Team. The monitoring team has to checkmate what is being executed; they are the ones to see if there will be a need for readjustment. Beyond this, this stage ensures that the

knowledge of climate change is relevant to what is being built or constructed. Not that alone, they must look into the hazard that is being faced and look keenly into what will happen shortly and how the design system features that. That isn't all; they have to be up-to-date with current information for deciding whether there will be an addition or subtraction.

Well, in some instance's adaptation might go wrong. It might be that what was hoped to bring relive, will further rain more havoc. Thus, it is vital that policies are well checked before execution, and if that is done, yet, it still results in a wreck, the stage starts all over again.

Also, another fear of adaptation is that when trying to avert problems from one community, it might be that other community having tranquility would now suffer while there is implementation, they will enjoy.

If that is the case, then those involved will now be opened to new information, allow contribution, and if there is a need for adjustment, they will do without delay.

And then, we can get quick asset that adaption doesn't appear as a goal; preferably it is a cycle or a process.

What can we summarize from this?

One, adaptation isn't simple as it may appear. Two, cooperation is essential for a better result- from private to public sector, new information must be gotten daily, new ways of designing solutions effectively must be obtained.

Finally, we can wrap it up by saying that any entity trying to adapt to climate change should know what particular climate impact they are waiting, what risk is involved, developing an adaptive strategy, implementing the verified plan and monitoring through the process of adaptation.

If these are done well, at least with a high degree of accuracy, every region will adapt well plus the effort to fight what leads to climate change.

Regardless of the stages of climate change adaptation, there are several techniques and ways to adapt, and this is for the individual. It is very evident that if all these stages are done rightly, they will bring reward to the team and all the citizens. Remember, all steps are critical and essential and must be critically looked into.

In adaptation options, there are varying reasons and foresight behind it. What are the goals? Journey with me as I bring the answer to the limelight.

### Reasons for Adaptation Options

From the previous subheading; you'd have seen that adaptation is solidly based on managing risk at all levels be it international, country wise or locals. The options then for adapting options is to bring benefits into improving the implementation. And since we've known that it is a cycle, many applications have to be developed.

And it is glaring that if adaptation techniques will be successful, it has to be thorough and be practical. Thus, adaptation option is classified into three aspects.

*1. Grey*

*2. Green*

*3. Soft Measures.*

1. For Grey Options. This section being the first adopts the two most vital aspects- technological and engineering solution to better the standard of people in the community. In implementing technical moves, what it does is to look for new technological innovations that can make the process smoother and easier. Granted technology races, and it's never stagnant. Thus, grey stage will always feature current actions, and the execution of unique aspect will give out practical ways of implementing it so that all members of the community are affected positively and not some set of people benefiting while others are not.

2 Green Stage. This stage is effectively based on eco-friendly implementation. And this stage is essential because it will not lead to other climate hazards. Slightly the improvising of green techniques will blend with the ecosystem and prove to be a solution indeed. That's not all; this stage applies several measures that the natural habitat provides so that they can comfortably improve the resilience and adaptation of the local community. And at this stage, if it's not green, it should not be implemented regardless of how promising it might be. Since the lack of green concept will led to other havocs that will creep in ultimately leading to more damage.

3. Soft Measures. The soft measure, which is the last category here involves financial measures, Social, policy, legal management that has the capability of influencing the pattern of governance and human behavior as a whole. This stage helps with creating awareness that will improve knowledge and other capacity involved.

As a result of these three categories. Adaption is then channeled at these aims below.

1. Admitting Impact and Bearing Losses. If it is evident that a climate change effect will set in, there should be no disguise, it will, and then if it will it will have to be based on bearing losses, then it should be done. For example, better techniques will be carved in managing retreat from sea level rise.

2. Offsetting Losses. Through insurance, it is possible to offset the loss. And this majorly includes spreading risks.

3. Avoiding Exposures to Climate Risk. It is true that adaptation is entirely different from mitigation, hence in adaptation too, you can change location, erect new structures that will combat the impact of climate change. Avoiding exposures as one of the aims of adaption options give individuals a better chance of having good health after a wreck. Some risks are higher than each other, therefore the higher the risk to be involved, then the quicker the decision to relocate or stay and build a defense.

4. Bringing About New Opportunity. Only when we can reduce human impact on climate change, then we can have peace of mind, that is when we can be confident that climate change, as it was happening a long time ago will happen naturally, but until then, adaptive options would cater for new possibilities, practices that will change into excellent conditions.

With these mentioned, adaptation options can also ensure the success of adaptation to climate change.

You'd recall that the types of adaptation techniques we discussed have more bearing on the government' addressing the issue to the betterment of the community. There are several processes individual and government can take up and implement.

I'll be discussing 10 of these practical ways.

**Ten practical Ways of Adapting to Climate Change.**

Just like mitigation, there are several ways of Adapting to Climate change, from farming to infrastructure and others.

Other wild geoengineering techniques are targeted at reversing climate change. They have proffer solution like storing excess carbon-dioxide or turning sunlight back into space. If you find this idea humorous, I do too! And this is because they won't still exempt us (humanity) from living admits climate change, decades to come. Meaning?

We must learn to adapt to! We must live with excess drought, and we must adapt to the rise in sea level, and many more. Adding to the humor, some adaptation techniques are based on high sci-fi imagination. Think, for example, model-like planting crops inside the city building, floating buildings and several other unrealistic methods of Adapting. All these would make the years of adaptation of humans longer, and as such, it would have a deviation from futuristic technology. Now with this adaption techniques to be discussed, will any of them feature this outrageous and unrealistic model? No!

Notwithstanding, some might seem like that to you, yet, all options here have been duly checked, and the basis for inclusion is reasonable and logical.

The first set of practical ways to apply are based on farming strategies, that is, how farmers can adapt well, some are based on infrastructures, and other includes what a random person can do, what skills they can carry out to implement the right adaptive strategy.

1. Share Practical Farming Tips. In some part of Africa, Ghana precisely, there was a time when farming practices was a lot easier. Much effort wasn't needed. Talking of adding nutrients and other essential things to improve yield only little effort was required, and when it's time for harvest, because of the excellent state of the land, they often have a bountiful harvest. But is that the same situation or has it improved? Why not hear from a local farmer, Clement Naazuin, who resides and is still farming in Ghana now, he said: "I have to put in extra soil nutrients." It is evident that several years of instability in the weather condition, from less rainfall to heat waves, other weather condition, and wind have a bearing on the yield of soil. But there is something worthwhile that is taking place in the country presently.

They are taking advantage of a process known as "Farmer Field School." This program is designed and developed by both governments and non-governmental organizations. This program has shown them innovative ways of adapting to Climate change. And how is Clement pointed out at the onset faring? He has been helping other farmers in his region to assist them in adjusting to Climate change.

That's not all, he has also been enjoying the benefit of composting, and this process requires zero or less capital. Most of the techniques used in the past like planting on the surface which makes plants more susceptible to erosion have been dropped, they've embraced a new method, that is making ridges. For some farmers in another district in the same country, Ghana, they are enjoying soil power, and this has improved their yield.

What's happening to farmers in Ghana has made it evident that new farming tips have to be shared if high yield wants to be maintained and they will be sure of better adaptation.

2. Pay Attention to Regional Communities. In some regions, this might be regarded as something new. However, it is of immense benefit. For example, in another African country, Kenya. They are now letting regional communities play a significant role in their implementation, decision making and executing solutions. While I'm picking Kenya in this regard is because its Kenya agricultural pattern rests on two different models; the agriculturists are based on crop farmers and nomadic pastoralists.

Surprisingly, when the government wanted to make decisions and policy regarding adaptation that will favor farmers, satisfying these two becomes a problem. To solve the problem and bridge the gap, they extend power to local governments to make decisions and after those decisions were reached to disburse adaptation fund to each region.

This decision will make the individual local community decide how they want to spend their fund, which adaptive techniques will be valid for them and will bring more yield.

This decision reached then worked out, and this is because regional communities know what is best for them. Do you wish to know how they carved our adaptive techniques? They used their fund in purchasing a radio station. Is this idea Realistic? Yes!

Most farmers have access to a radio, thus giving out information about weather situation will keep all farmers updated. They are ahead, and for some farmers who at that time doesn't have one, they will definitely have access to it. Isn't that an excellent idea? I'll leave the answer to you!

3. Making Judicious Use of Social Network. Social Networking? Yes! It's high time Farmers up their game. Or what do you think, if some farmer can think of an adaptive strategy that includes the use of a radio station? Which other technological advancements would not be reachable for farmers who are willing to learn and who are bent on doing things the right way? I doubt if there will be.

Farmers who are tech-savvy and who are ready to outwit climate change and are prepared to adapt well should be prepared to purchase a smartphone. This will assist them in getting data news about the changing climate. This information gives them weather forecast, although it can't be 100% relied on, most of the prediction is right. Also, in an African country where a website like Young Volunteers for Environment is made public, farmers in that country can have access to weather updates in their region, where they live.

And being sure what is to be expected is invaluable. For instance, the difference between failed harvest and good yield lies in knowing how much precipitation is expected and when it will rain.

There is more to the opportunities that farmers in this country enjoy. Aside from the frequent update of weather, they rely on specific and practical tips about how and when to plant a particular crop in expectation of a climate change. And tell me, how would farmers not adapt well in this kind of situation?

It's certain that developed countries like the United States and the United Kingdom have a more sophisticated mode of informing farmers about expected weather situation, and the level of accuracy will be higher than in developing countries because they have access to more funds for updates and more firsthand use of technology-based information.

Caution for some farmers in developing lands is that they should have a proper view of the internet and the use of a gadget that can access it. One, the type of cell phones to buy does not necessarily have to be expensive, two, most of the credits of Forecast should not be engraved in superstitious believe, they must embrace it as part of the world development experience.

Any attempt to look down on these processes, then, adapting in the best way will be a problem, which will have a deadly blow on the food supply of the land and if not attempts are even made to mitigate, massive imbalance of the ecosystem and difficult in surviving is inevitable.

4. Implementing Long Term Planning from Decision Makers. Policy makers or decision makers should believe that regular implementation is needed and adding to that they must adapt to their techniques to ensure that they have excellent skill coping with their environment that is even very unpredictable. Let's use an incidence that happened in the past in giving a clear narration of what policymakers should be up to.

In the Himalayan State of Uttarakhand, there occurs a disheartening flood that hits the state which claimed the lives of about more than 5000 inhabitants, if that were enough, the damage would still have been endurable, but it went further, so many infrastructures, public and private were destroyed. What would top policymaker say or how will they react? The chief minister pledges to execute development differently. Is the word meant at the right time? Or should he have worked on the cause long before now? We gain an answer to that from an environmentalist.

He criticized the minister and said further that the disaster that happened as a result of the Tunnels that were blasted through the Himalaya to channel water to and for the successful completion of the construction of the hydroelectric dam. And did the minister learn from what happened?

Happily, he did. He found the need to establish sustainable thinking. To that effect, he did what will be of benefit to nearly everyone around in the country. He created the Relief and Reconstruction Authority. This is a great way to develop an adaptive strategy.

But we are still left to learn a few things about the program he established? Yes. The program aims to ensure that future planning of the country's construction projects. The sets of people must include Environmentalists, geologists, and scientists.

Though a sad way to learn, it is still pretty better than not Learning at all. This small incident related teaches the core lesson. It helps to see that at all levels, governments should implement long term planning. They have to include people who are experts as regards the study of the climate into their policies and development.

Also, before any project is executed, these set of people, environmentalists and scientists should be called to add their input, what the structure would mean to the region or what benefit they hope to achieve.

5. Prepare Well in Advance. Some regions might not be able to do much than to adapt to climate change that will occur in their neighborhood. This knowledge would necessitate adequate preparedness. How to prepare begins from the warning. Dwellers of such regional should receive notices in advance. That is, if a weather forecast suggests that in near time, there will be excess rainfall, this information should adequately circulate the region, and what they need to about it, but is that all?

No. Excess rainfall leading to flooding will lead to displacement of properties and live in severe cases. Thus, knowing about it has no sufficiency in itself. There must be designing of structures in areas far from the expected hazards. The shelter will serve as a refuge for those that will be affected.

Aside from the shelter, the government should also be ready to give instructions on what to do in advance before the set date. This reduces the cost of handling the situation. How?

Assume that we have just four regions in a community - Region A, B, C, D. But among these regions, region C is expected to experience a change in precipitation- high rate of rainfall. Governments are informed. Thus, they created shelters for an inhabitant of region C-where the said incident is said to occur in Region D- the closest area where housing could be sort.

The government knew the date the incident is said to occur. Then they order all the those who reside in region C to vacate the region in a set date - which is one week ahead of the occurrence. They could even provide them logistics to move their belongings. But think about this with this warning in advance, do you think the government will have to give each person food and clothing? No!

They've left before the incident, and surely, they would have made provisions for that.

So only a few losses would be recorded. They would have catered for their drinking, safe drinking ability, all this planning need smartness. Readiness to serve the people and have their interests at heart. If governments at all level would always put their citizens at heart, they can have reward and enjoy the benefit.

Finally, we have to make drastic changes now, because climate change is set to occur more and more shortly and with more tools to cope with an increase in population, better infrastructure put in place, there will be adequate adapting.

6. Water world Homes. What would happen in the future when the water level has an increase, tomorrow 's building may rise too and though it turns out to be a floating structure.

This is a real concern for everyone. Thus, this has pushed the head of Waterstudio.Nl, Koen Olthuis to begin working on projects of floating apartments. One in the Netherlands and other in the United Arab Emirates. In conjunction with that, the Netherlands organizations have also designed several floating hotels, different types of buildings and several company's hall in the Maldives island found in the India country. But why is this structure needed for adaptability?

If you are current with world news, you would recall that this area is expected to hit and a total submission in the year 2080. If you check the statement well, it didn't just say flooding will start troubling the region by 2080," rather it means that total submission will end by the year 2080. We can learn that the problem would begin in a few decades to come. Hence, the design of these structures is mandatory.

Is this feasible? Yes. Dura Vermeer, at a pioneering Dutch firm, has made floating buildings, and they are greenhouses. Thus, they incorporate the ecosystem into the design. What are some of the features?

The building has many layers that are made of foams; these layers are then formed into floating grids. These grids are designed to support concrete structures. And when traced back to the olden days. Something incredible was noticed.

It was gathered that in the ancient time, in Bangladesh, homes were built on silt which aided floating on water.

Now, countries who have some of their communities near water and who are at risk of the high level of sea rise in nature should ensure that they improvise. By adopting this design, they can put the safety of their citizens in check. Nevertheless, there might be laws governing individual structures. Thus, before any government of the world agree to design structures, they can further inquire everything about the structure and how they can fair in the long run. Irrespective of whatever is believed in any state or country, this design is gaining prominence now, and it is offering a great way to adapt.

7. Underground Cities. Before you laugh at this, allow me to tell you about underground cables. Remember that in a bit to fight power outages from the impact of climate change. Some electricity cables have been buried underground in lands where they are a low risk of landslide and earthquake. This step has benefited the resident of these towns. They have been enjoying uninterrupted electricity even in the face of a severe storm in sharp contrast to those who still have their cables spread outside in the atmosphere. What do you think?

Building houses underground, is it a failed idea, or a dead or arrival approach? We need for further learning.

This project is far from a wishful dream nor does the idea seems ugly and unappealing. Preferably, it is a design technique that provides humans incredible safety from severe weather condition. Life underground should be seen as a pastoral paradise and profoundly different from what it might be in films.

Let's dig further into the benefits of this infrastructure. For example, despite our adaptation to the sunlight rays. Living underground will protect us and screen out ultraviolet rays that are harmful to our body.

For concerns for plants life, a fiber optic capable could be designed to transfer light and supply light into the underground region to provide food for trees and allow plants to grow well. The electric lightning too can make it possible for everyone to see the light during night time or when it is cloudy.

Undoubtedly, this solution will have a far-reaching effect. It will give more protection to both man and plants. There will be better since plants will grow in their most favorable condition; also, they will have to be free from pest and insect that can destroy the plants causing a shortage in the food made available for us.

Admittedly, this isn't somewhat like a small project. If started at a global scale, the government's permission for acquisition of land might be needed. One of the fears of this policy is acceptance by decision makers. If approved, it is delighted that there will be laws that will be governing thorough use of that kind of facility. Right though, it would be an expensive undertaken. Therefore, governments can invest fund into these and then lease to people at a subsidized rate. Thus, many people can gain access to comfort and luxury. Thus, even if climate change continues, adapting will become easier.

8. Floating Farm. If in the region you live, there is little the government of that land is doing in a dressing climate change. Then, they've not been made to learn in a hard way - must we learn the hard way?

Unfortunately, Bangladesh had to learn in a hard way. How did it happen? About 140million people in the region of Bangladesh has been forced to live with climate change in a hard way. And see, in this region much of the land available in the area are approximately 15 ft above sea level.

More sad incidents are happening. Flood covers 1/4 of the country in a mean year and over 60% every four to five years. And what has this taught Bangladesh residents? Development of floating agriculture!

This adaptation techniques that help one to live in a world of constant rising sea and extreme cases of flooding. So how did they go about that to help the world at large learn about it?

What they did was building floating rafts from straw, rice stubble and water hyacinth, after that, they now added decomposing water Worts to serve as manure. As a result of these techniques and design, the raft, in turn, becomes free-floating surfaces that now serve as an alternative to floated agricultural land. It doesn't just serve as an alternative but has provided more yield and has even shown more crops than traditional fields would.

So, it's even a better alternative! What a profitable way of adapting. What do you learn from this? It is not until when tragedy strikes before we take drastic steps.

If the steps are to be taken now, do and reap the benefits. Although the city of Bangladesh is enjoying the adaptive strategy, it's obvious they regretted delayed in adaptation. Now in the region you live can this type of design feature. Are there areas that are often prone to flood? If you don't know, are you ready to make changes that are relevant and would require implementation by the government.

Make an inquiry and see if this pattern has already taken effect in your country if it hasn't can you relate it to firms that are charged with the monitoring of the environment? Or, in turn, they can explain to top officials, and thus they see if there are resources for that and then implement it.

9. Vertical Farms. With a warmer climate, there are more expectations of drought hitting more farmers and also there will be more pest infesting their produce. And to solve the problem, one design has already started, this design is becoming a widely accepted form of farm cultivation now across the world.

These vertical farms consist of several layers that are aligned to the skyward and even underground.

It has been experimented that crops grown in an open field might be less efficient to this space saving setup. This is because it provides an indoor regulated climate to raise crops. Is your country set for this development?

Gladly many have been responding to this vertical farm. For example, regions like Sweden, Japan, the United States, and the Netherlands have started experimenting the efficiency in their vertical farms.

This technique is an excellent way to build an agricultural sector that is more resilient and adaptive. This also will increase more crop yield and great growing of crops.

Either you are a farmer or not you can benefit from this development. Write a letter, meet top officials and relate these highly effective ways of adapting to Climate in the environment. Some animals would even benefit efficiently from this setup and planning.

10. Climate-Adapted Crops. There is a need to divert attention from crops susceptible to climate change to Climate-Adapted crops. Well, know this, vegetables do not have to be moved indoors before it survives. What they need is how perfectly they adapt to shifting in temperature and drought.

For example, there is a species of corn called drought-resistant crop. These types of plants are excellent in growing in areas where there is less water, and they've been out for sale from several countries. For much agricultural business, they've disbursed millions of dollars into climate reduction crops that are capable of withstanding heat, flooding, and cold.

Nevertheless, without genetic engineering, if unique traits in existing crops are studied, that could also be regarded as climate change adaptation.

What every government in every land should learn to do is to make these species of crops available to the masses. Additionally, they should buy and invest more money into these techniques. Since genetic engineering isn't the only way, if more studies are done into the crops planted in several regions, they could verify if they have several adaptive techniques.

Finally, on this adaptation. Recall we started from what adaptation is, and we've seen that natural adaption has been in existence for a very long time. And with the advent of drastic climate change, things have changed. And that means, a more comprehensive way of adapting needs to be designed. More designed for animals, plants and humans must be developed.

Yes, we need mitigation, but that isn't sufficient, adaptation is required at all level. From international level down to the local level.

At this stage where we've discussed all climate changes impact, the mitigation techniques and lastly adaptation to climate change. Thus, what can we conclude?

That leads us to the final face of this book. The part that sums up all you've learned.

# Conclusion

Distinctly, you have come a long way! Isn't it rewarding? Aren't you glad to have read so immense about climate change? Satisfactorily, this book has helped you in acquiring knowledge from the smallest part of climate change to the intricate part; you aren't a novice to the concept of climate and climate change itself, you've obtained modern ways of solving climate change, and you now know better the facts surrounding it. Isn't it? At this point, let us have a brief recap!

You have read extensively on how climate change affects human existence, how it affects, food, air, temperature and the specific populations that it impacts, and you saw how these impacts have led to displacement. Conclusively on that chapter, you have seen what individuals could do about the implications on human existence. It will be gratifying if we all adhere to that.

On the impact on animals, you've seen why you should care, you have seen how climate change leads to animal migration, I've related some of the species affected by climate change and you have seen the way climate change could lead to their extinction, in the worst case scenario, what human-activities has resulted, and more than ever before why we should pay usual attention to climate change and adopting an eco-friendly environment.

Furthermore, this book has discussed the impact of climate change on water, how sea life is being affected, how water cycle has been impacted, why there seems to be the imbalance between water supply and water demand. Concisely, I have highlighted how freshwater security will be affected, and how to redeem the impact climate change wrecks on water. You have verified with available facts and data featured in this book on how climate change has led to several alterations in the habitat of sea life, how it has affected their ecosystem, their food chain and how it has influenced them to migrate.

You have equally seen how agriculture sets to be affected by climate change, the effects on crops, effects on plants, effects on livestock, fisheries, what several technological options are made available and sufficiently, what agro-ecology solves.

In the economy as well, you've learned that climate change can impact the economy of an individual country and how it can affect the global economy. Even though some argues that it can't, gaining detailed explanation into the continent of Europe has given more insight into and has shown that it is possible. You now better understand what growth zones are and how industry, technology and several other concepts of the economy are impacted.

The energy of the world is also a crucial aspect that has been extensively discussed, you have seen how storm surge, water availability, sea level life, and wind affect the quality of electricity received. Moreover, we have seen what you can do to ensure more demands are off the non-renewable power supply, and how shifts could be made to the renewable power supply.

We have seen that climate change can impact the changing of seasons. That is how season changes, and how it affects the shift in seasons.

The final part on how to fight climate change - mitigation and how to cope with the risk involved - adaptation have been heavily discussed with more examples from several countries and regions. We have seen that even though adaptation not checked into, we must all give concern to that.

Don't forget that differences in impact will differ from region to region, also, while some areas will record some loss, some might record gains. Regardless, climate change is often keen about destroying lives, infrastructure, and the ecosystem.

Finally, if the emission of carbon gasses continues, then the fighting of climate change will be futile. Governments have a formidable task to ensure that people, industries comply with environmental standards. Regardless, as an individual, you must strive to put a halt on the amount of carbon you emit.

Several options have been discussed in this book; they work for both individual and government so that they can reduce the emission of carbon into the atmosphere. The possibilities discussed have their risks too, they demand dispensation of money into the process and having the relevant and specific human resources needed in the execution of the solutions. Also, techniques of adaptation discussed should be looked into by every interested person that is keen about how to survive these hazards.

Also, before any individual or government picks any of the options in this book, it has to be critically checked to know if it will be beneficial to them or if the implementation will not require the solution for the regions.

Also, it has to be noted that before government plans on erecting a construction projects scientists, environmentalist and in some cases geologist has to be included in the process, and they have to check into the effectiveness of such structure, if it can affect or impact the ecosystem and trigger natural disaster.

The scientific description of climate change discussed in this book is opened for the use of the public and governmental use to enable them to carve policies that will better the health and general well-being of their citizens.

Also, the effort to maintain a favorable climate isn't just about the government alone, rather, it is everyone's effort.

The book - "Climate Change- the facts, impacts and remedies" has related, shown facts from country to country, conferences, scientific data, and it has impressively discussed the impact as explained above and finally it has extensively examined the remedies that would be needed in rectifying the damages or halting future damage that might come underway. Honestly, the book is the gateway to facts, the reveler of impacts and the solution to the hazards it brings.

# About the Author

Sachin's first two books are:

***Climate Change:*** The Facts, Impacts and Remedies

***Artificial Intelligence:*** How It Changes the Future

These can be found as E-books as well as paperback.